I Love You. Now Go Away

Confessions of a Woman with a Smartphone

Dawn Weber

Beetle Hill Books

I LOVE YOU. NOW GO AWAY:

CONFESSIONS OF A WOMAN WITH A SMARTPHONE

Copyright © 2016 by Dawn Weber

Author's note: The events described in this book are mostly true, though some timelines have been compressed, and some stories exaggerated and satirized for comedic effect. To protect anonymity, some characters have been combined, and names and identifying characteristics have been changed.

Acknowledgment is made to the following, in which essays from this book first appeared, possibly differently titled or in slightly different form: *You Have Lipstick On Your Teeth: And Other Things You'll Only Hear from Your Friends In the Powder Room* (PRG Media, 2013): "There's an App for That. Yes—That"; *Not Your Mother's Book: On Being a Mom* (Publishing Syndicate LLC, 2014): "The Family That Raps Together Stays Together"; *Car Bombs to Cookie Tables: The Youngstown Anthology* (Belt Publishing, 2015): "Hiding the Evidence. It's a Youngstown Thing."

Cover design by Vanessa Maynard

ISBN: 978-0-692-78908-7

'Dawn Weber wrote this book on her smartphone. My smartphone has a dumb owner, so I read it on my computer. Either way, it's hilarious. In '*I Love You. Now Go Away*,' Dawn captures the craziness of family life with sassy, laugh-out-loud humor. If I can figure out how to text, I'll get on my smartphone and tell her how much I enjoyed it."

— Jerry Zezima, syndicated humor columnist for *The Stamford Advocate* and author of "*Leave It to Boomer*," "*The Empty Nest Chronicles*" and "*Grandfather Knows Best*"

CONTENTS

For the Husband, the Princess and the Hobo,
as well as my mother, who pretty much patented the phrase
"I love you. Now go away" during the 70s. I get it now, Mom.
I get it.

INTRODUCTION
Sunday, 7:32 a.m.

Psstt. Come over here. I'll tell you a secret.

I do it on the bleachers. I do it in cars, at stores, and in parking lots during broad daylight.

I do it on my phone.

No, no. Not that, you perv. What I do is write. I write everywhere, and all the time. In fact, I wrote the book—on a cell phone.

Yeah, you read that right, this book was written on a smartphone. At sporting events, between errands, in the bathroom—anywhere I could, I grabbed my trusty phone and punched away, tapping out more than 59,000 words on a 3.5" screen.

I'm pretty much blind now. Also, I have thumb arthritis.

The whole thing was an accident. A while back, whenever something ridiculous happened, I wanted to get it off my chest by expressing myself. This was nothing new; I'm always expressing myself.

Just ask my husband.

But these were stories, people and ridiculous scenes from life that I felt the need to capture somewhere in precious minutes of alone time, before it all vanished into the frazzled ether of a middle-aged mind. I craved nothing more than a few quiet minutes to sit, write this stuff down, and just be, because for me, solitude is the new sex. I think about it constantly, crave it all the time and never, ever get any.

Then, right at my fingertips, I found a way to deal with the frustrating lack of solo writing time: my smartphone. Beeping and buzzing with emails, texts, Tweets and Facebook updates, it demanded my constant attention anyway. Why not use it for something constructive?

So these days, I don't get mad—I get mobile. When I'm surrounded by

1

pesky, challenging people or outrageous situations, wherever I am, with whatever spare time available, I whip this phone out, and I take names.

Not only did I write *I Love You. Now Go Away* on a smartphone, I designed it to be easily read on one, with brief chapters that can be finished in short time spans during a bus commute or a halftime. They're stories you'd share with your BFFs, your office mates, or your fellow football moms, stuck beside you in the cubicles or on the bleachers for hours on end.

People sometimes ask why I wrote an entire book on a phone. The simple truth is I had much to say, and it was the only means available. Plus, I don't want to limit my thoughts to the internet—I enjoy sharing my valuable opinion.

Just ask my husband.

Anyway, why not write a book on a smartphone? The list of tasks you can accomplish with these devices is endless: You can pay bills, watch TV, start your car—you can do anything on a smartphone nowadays. And I do mean anything. Wait until you get to chapter 55.

How's that for foreshadowing?

CHAPTER ONE
Presidents Day, Veterans Day—For the Love of God, Go to School
Monday, 7:42 a.m.

I love you. Now go away.

No, no, no. I'm not talking to you. I'm talking to my children.

Mother of the Year, right here.

I only want them to go on Monday—my one day alone, my only day off. My sole day here in the house without kids, without stress, without endless requests for food, drinks or money. A day of 1,000 chores, yes, but of 1,000 chores I accomplish in peace and solitude. Complete and wonderful solitude.

I work four 10-hour days, so my weekends are spent—as they should be—with and for the kids, chauffeuring, cleaning, cooking. That leaves me with one day free, and oh, how I look forward to Mondays. I look forward to no one needing a drink, a meal, some cash, a ride. I look forward to no one needing anything.

I look forward to no one needing me.

There's just one problem. On average, two Mondays out of four each month, I hear heartbreaking words—sad, hopeless phrases that fill me with despair:

"No school Monday! Teacher's meeting!"

"No school Monday! District conferences!"

"No school Monday! It's Presidents Day/Veterans Day/Memorial Day!"

Now, don't get me wrong; I love being a mom. I do. Nothing is more fulfilling, more wonderful, more maddening, more all-encompassing, more blissful, than motherhood.

But on Mondays, I like to do my chores, then kick back and pursue my dreams. You know—shop for shoes online, take a nap, maybe open up a nice box of wine.

New shoes, nap, box of wine. Folks, that is pretty much as good as it gets.

I pondered all this last Monday at 7:30 a.m., having some quality writing time with my phone in my thinking place. It was Presidents Day—of course it was—so the kids were off school again—of course they were—and I'd awakened early, trying to squeeze in an hour or two of tranquility before it all began. My plan was to fix a cup of coffee, get some writing done, have a nice sit-down there in the bathroom . . .

Doh!

The bathroom! No! What was I thinking? How could I forget that my presence there sounds an automatic alarm for those two? Even the quietest noises made in the can trigger a child's sonic-bat-hearing, signaling to their wee brains that they need immediate assistance. Why did I do it? Why did I think I could have ten minutes to myself?

I haven't had ten minutes to myself since the Bush administration. The first one.

Maybe they hadn't heard me. Maybe I would get lucky this time. I quietly reached for the flush handle, pushed it down carefully, carefully . . .

Thump, thump, thump.

Too late.

Here they came, down the steps, immediately appearing outside the door. Tousled hair, rumpled pajamas, they looked adorable—and somehow evil—their devious little minds already at work with requests. God made them cute for a purpose, and that purpose is survival.

Ah yes—happy Presidents Day. My fate was sealed. I put down the phone, washed my hands, and turned to face both kids.

"What's-for-breakfast-would-you-pour-me-some-chocolate-milk-can-Logan-come-over?" asked my son, the Hobo, in his trademark mismatched clothes.

"I-don't-want-cereal-what-else-do-we-have-can-you-give-me-some-money-would-you-take-me-and-my-friends-to-the-mall?" demanded my daughter, the Princess.

So I poured chocolate milk. I called Logan's mom. I made some eggs. I drove girls to the mall, forked over cash and I spent the rest of the day chauffeuring, cleaning and cooking.

And it was all fine, because a small flame of hope flickered in my heart. I knew that next Monday, those two would possibly, maybe, just perhaps go to school.

Blessed school.

The week went by, as it does when one is breathing, and it flew, as it does when one is busy.

Monday has returned. I awaken and smile to myself, because the house feels still. There are no teacher's meetings, no district conferences; it is not Presidents Day, Veterans Day or Memorial Day.

I stretch, yawn, roll over, and I see:

The husband. He's awake, staring at me, grinning at me.

I do not return his grin. "What are you doing here?"

"I had some vacation days I had to use or lose, so I took today off."

I slap my hand to my forehead, covering my eyes. "Please tell me you're kidding!"

"I thought you'd be happy!" he says.

"I'm not happy!"

This does not deter him. He snuggles closer. "Mmm. You feel good. You wanna?"

"No! I don't wanna," I say, jumping from the bed.

He follows me toward the bathroom, pouting. "You don't love me anymore!"

"Yes I do!" I yell, slamming the door behind me.

Of course I do. We've been together 20 years. I'm still here, aren't I?

I adore you. I need you. I live for you—all that happy horseshit. I most certainly love you.

But I will love you more if you go away.

At least, on Mondays.

5

CHAPTER TWO
Toilet Paper. Is It Too Much to Ask? Yes, Apparently
Wednesday, 5:30 p.m.

I dream of a place.

A quiet place where I can sit down, relax, write—have a little me-time. A peaceful place where all my needs are met and I have everything required to meet my needs.

This time, I think, things will be different, and I will find my place. I will settle back, take a load off, without a worry, without a care—really let myself go.

So I sit. I settle in. But it is not to be. Because I turn my head left, and I see it:

Cardboard.

Spool.

Empty TP roll.

Children: squashing my dreams since 1997.

It's a metaphor for parenting, really. Just as in life, kids use it all up, and leave you with none. They take and take and give you nothing, bleed you dry. Or wet, as the case may be.

Now I have to do the old TP shuffle, and waddle, pants around the ankles, across the room, through the kitchen, down some stairs, possibly out to the trunk of the car, looking for Charmin.

I blame my boobs for this. I'm pretty sure my mammies have granted me superpowers, because I am the only one in this family capable of accomplishing certain things. No one else here has a grown-up set of beanbags, and no one else can do the things I do. I am special, and not in a need-to-wear-a-helmet kind of way.

It's mind-blowing, the superhuman feats I manage around here that nobody else can, thanks to my blinkers. You see those, in the kitchen? The mountain of cups and mugs on the counter? I am the sole person capable of lifting and loading them into the dishwasher, such is the strength of my breasts. And look, there in the fridge! The leftovers? I am the only one capable of covering them with Saran Wrap, so that they remain edible and free of dog hair.

Of all the Super Amazing Life Skills the fun-bags have granted me, perhaps the greatest are my Toilet Paper Replacement Powers. So I decided to share them with the children of America. It's a public service, really. What can I say? I'm a giver. All in the day's work of a superhero.

Toilet Paper Replacement Super-Procedure:

1. Make sure that you're settled in, half naked and releasing bodily fluids before checking TP situation. Turn head and see: cardboard.

2. Cuss. Like a filthy sailor.

3. Rise from the toilet. Ensure pants are wrapped around the ankles, and whatever you were excreting drips swiftly down your legs.

4. Shuffle awkwardly to bathroom cupboard, open, and peer in: Drano, Tampax, Comet cleanser. But no toilet paper. Not even a box of tissues.

5. Cuss. Like a filthy sailor.

6. Yell, "Can someone bring me a roll of mother-&*^($%**# toilet paper!" Repeat several times. Then remember that you're the only one home.

7. Waddle out to kitchen, hoping, at this point, that you truly are the only one home, because the dripping situation has reached bio-hazard proportions. Check cupboards and pantry for TP. Nothing. Not even a napkin.

8. Lurch awkwardly out, out, out to the garage. Realizing family is due home any minute, glance furtively at garage door and pray it doesn't rise. Pop the car's trunk, and grab pack of Charmin forgotten from last week's trip to Walmart.

9. Shuffle—quickly now!—back in, in, in to the bathroom.

10. Sit.

11. Remove wrapper, obtain fresh roll of paper, and—kids of America, I beseech you, this is key—slide empty cardboard spool off TP spindle.

12. Slide fresh roll of paper on spindle. If you're not too tired from all this effort, reach two inches behind you and throw empty cardboard away.

13. Wipe. Relax. Glance down at streaked legs, and realize you now need a shower.

14. Cuss. Like a filthy, filthy sailor.

With this handy Toilet Paper Replacement Super-Procedure, I hope to help all American children obtain the powers possessed by those of us with magical mammies. I'd like to especially dedicate these instructions to my own two kids, who, sadly, didn't inherit my Super Amazing Life Skills. A wise, wise woman named Whitney Houston once said that children are our future, that we should teach them well, let them lead the way.

Print these instructions out, kids. They'll teach you well. They will let you lead the way. Mom is a superhero, however, she isn't going to live forever, and after she's gone, life will be difficult. You'll feel frightened, sad. You'll feel lonely, grief-stricken and lost.

But . . .

. . . you'll still need to wipe.

CHAPTER THREE
I Thought I Looked MILF-ish. I'm Told I Was Wrong
Thursday, 6:39 p.m.

My kids call me names. And not nice ones.

But I fancy myself most MILF-ish tonight, sitting here in the restaurant parking lot, waiting to meet up with my family. I have on a nice new outfit—a green silk shirt, black pants, and kitten-heel shoes, both made of velvet.

A word about velvet: I absolutely *love* it. In a perfect world, *everything* would be made of velvet, all clothing, car interiors, cubicle walls, and especially lingerie. Personally, I've been on a 20-year mission to find panties made of velvet. My home-boy George Costanza (a.k.a. Art Vandelay, a.k.a. Lord of the Idiots) of *Seinfeld* said it best:

"I'd *drape* myself in velvet if it was socially acceptable!'

Mmmm. Velvet.

Wait—I had a point here. What was it? Oh yeah.

So I figure I'm looking pretty shag-worthy, definitely velvety, also I'm truly excited about endless baskets of tortilla chips as my husband and children pull up beside me in the Honda. We exit the vehicles, lock up, then begin walking into Central Ohio's finest "No habla Ingles" strip mall restaurant.

"Hey, guys," I say, smiling. "I'm *so* hungry."

My children turn, eyeing me up and down. Obviously, they admire the velvet.

"You like my new outfit, don't you? It's velvet!"

For some reason, they clap their hands over their mouths, widen their eyes and begin laughing.

"Well," chokes the girl, between guffaws, "Your shirt looks like a

9

grandma shirt!"

"And your shoes look like elf shoes!" giggles the boy.

They double over and shake with silent laughter. The boy raises his head first.

"Hey, you're a . . . a . . . a *grelf*!"

"What?" I ask.

"A grandma-elf!"

Can you feel the love?

I'm going for "MILF." I get "grelf."

From my son, the Hobo, named as such because he avoids personal hygiene and dresses himself like a crackhead.

And my daughter, the Princess, fond of spending all our money on grossly overpriced name-brand T-shirts and hoodies. She generally dresses like some kind of Abercrombie track-and-field team member.

Neither wears velvet of any sort. I don't know what's wrong with them. Evidently, they didn't inherit my mad fashion skills.

But they're good at nicknames, and proud of this fact. I watch as they whip out their phones and iPods and program me in as "Grelf Weber."

Grelf is not the only new name I've received around here lately. No sir. Do not underestimate my family's ability to insult me.

One night not long ago, it was pretty late—7 p.m. and all—so I was in the house wearing my usual post-work attire of pajama bottoms and a cami-shirt.

For those of you senior citizens and Grelfs-like-me out there, what the young folks call a "cami" is a spaghetti-strap tank top, usually with a makeshift built-in bra inside. I love to sleep in them, because I tend to get very hot under the covers.

I also love the little bra-contraption in such tops; they allow aging mammies a modicum of support, without the choking rib-strangulation of a regular brassiere. I have several dozen camis, even one made of—wait for it—velvet.

Mmmm. Velvet.

Wait, where was I? Oh yeah.

I forgot I was wearing a cami that night, when I heard a car coming up the driveway to bring my daughter home from practice.

"That's probably the Corsis," I told the husband. "I should go out and say hi."

He glanced over at me from the kitchen table, then looked me up and down.

"You better put on a sweatshirt, Halter Hattie," he said. "You can see their headlights—they don't need to see yours."

Halter Hattie. Halter-fucking-Hattie.

I spun around to face him.

"'Halter Hattie'? This is *not* a halter top—it's a cami," I said. "Thanks a lot. Halter Hattie? Now I feel old, white trash, and, like, saggy at the same time. Halter Hattie?! Why don't you just go get me a 40-ounce and a pack of Pall Malls?"

I flounced outside to talk to my friends, but first I grabbed a sweatshirt, because—true enough—the particular rigging in camis does not leave much to the imagination in the chest region.

You've seen a woman in a cami? You've pretty much seen her naked boobies.

But that is no reason to call her names. At least without bringing her a 40-ounce and a pack of Pall Malls first. Or some velvet.

And judging by the names they call me lately, my family sees me as old.

You know what? I'll give them old. I'll give them ancient. And deaf:

"Hey Mommy—can I go over to Evan's house?"

"Mom. Can you make me a hair appointment for homecoming?"

"Honey? What's for dinner?"

What's that? Sorry, folks. I do not understand this "Mom/Mommy/Honey" of whom you speak.

I only answer to Grelf. Or Halter Hattie.

CHAPTER FOUR
I'm Not Coming Out of the Closet. I Have My Reasons
Saturday, 1:22 p.m.

Looking for a certain purse in the closet just now, I came across my emergency bag of chocolate chips.

I can't find the purse. But I really don't care.

No, I do not. I grab that bag, lock the bedroom door, sit down on my shoes, lean back against the adjustable shelves and have a little Nestle me-time.

Yeah, I keep baking supplies in my bedroom closet. Don't you? Doesn't everybody? It's where they go, tucked amongst wallets and belts and jeans, hidden safely away from everyone. That is just the kind of loving, generous person I am.

These chips are there for me in times of adversity—difficult, sorrowful events, such as PMS, weekday mornings and the Trying on of Pants.

I chew slowly, savoring each bite. I eat chips instead of candy bars, because it's easier to manage portion sizes that way, since I don't have any sort of self-control. While eating, I think of all the good times here in my closet, where I might possibly also store some cookies at Christmas, a tub of frosting during the summer—maybe a bottle of wine when certain relatives visit.

Do not judge me.

Emergency sugar, emergency wine—whatever. It's the secret bomb shelter of a middle-aged woman.

True, my closet is too small for clothes. But its size makes it a great mini-vacation for one—nobody bothering me in here, asking for things, taking my chocolate. It could use something in the way of cookie dough, so I'm thinking of putting in a little fridge, perhaps a wet bar. The conversation pit will go over there, past the Nikes.

I post news of my closeted ways to Facebook here from my phone, and I soon find out I'm not alone. My friend Mechelle says she keeps fun-size candy bars in hers. Becky comments that hidden icing makes a fine accompaniment to hidden chocolate chips—along with a necessary hidden spoon—and says her best friend Lisa has also been known to hide wine, although Lisa denies this. "It's Wild Turkey," she says. "I don't drink wine."

Yes, all across the U.S. of A., women are in the closet. If they're smart.

You want some chocolate chips? Too damn bad.

They're all mine and I don't want to share and any person desiring my chocolate should first acquire written permission from, say, the governor. That's why my candy goes in the closet, and also for two other reasons: husband and daughter reasons.

Chocolate is their crack. Doesn't matter whose it was originally—they think it's theirs, and before you can say "diabetes," it's gone. They'll steal it, then scarf it, just like a couple of crackheads.

I have no idea where they get this tendency.

They're especially adept at swiping my son's Halloween candy, after he spends hours walking the hills of our hometown, simultaneously sweating and freezing and shouting, "Trick or treat!" from his plastic Walmart mask. No sooner does that boy walk through the door before he's swooped and shoved aside, his pumpkin pilfered for any signs of cocoa beans.

Reese's cups are the first to go, wrappers crumbled before Batman gets his shoes off. Then the crackheads take the Twix, the Milky Ways, the Snickers. Last are the Hershey bars—plain, true, but easy for an addict to dip in a jar of peanut butter.

Black cape askew, the boy struggles to his feet to assess what they've left him . . . Necco wafers, Sweet Tarts, sad, raggedy Dum Dums. He scoops up the violated pumpkin and loser leftovers, and brings them to me, so we can hide the remains.

Come, little Batman, I shall save you from the junkies. My closet's warm. There's chocolate and a change of clothes and even a little wine if certain relatives are visiting.

Do you have chocolate crackheads at your place? Before taking candy anywhere near them, ask yourself: Do I want this? Because there's a good chance they will cut you to get it.

Clearly, the wisest course of action for you is to turn over all your chocolate, your candy, your cookie dough, maybe your wine—to me. For safekeeping. I'll stash it securely, right here by my purses, shoes and pants.

You know—the pants that no longer fit.

CHAPTER FIVE
I Don't Always Get My Kids' Texts on My Phone. But When I Do I Read Them All
Thursday, 8:38 p.m.

The Hobo has a girlfriend. He's not happy about it. It wasn't his decision.

But he does.

I know this because I can see his text messages here on my phone. He also wouldn't be happy about that, if he knew. But he doesn't yet. And I can.

My son, age 10, received an iPod touch for his birthday, and downloaded free texting software that he can use on wifi.

Now, please understand: I don't go around reading my kids' text messages. I try to—repeatedly. But they lock their screens.

The other night, while searching Pinterest for Mason jar uses, my phone pinged with a weird new notification, saying I had messages. I touched the weird thing, and there, in all their glory, were the text communications between my son and his "girlfriend."

I soon figured out that since the Hobo's iPod is linked to my email account, his texting app appeared on my device—with messages intact.

Mommy - 1, Hobo - 0.

The "girlfriend" in question is my daughter's good friend, and I'll call her "Lily", to protect the "innocent." And because I like the name "Lily" and it's my "damn book."

Lily's a polite, beautiful, popular, 15-year-old, so it's very easy to imagine why someone like her would want to date my 10-year-old hobo. He's handsome and sweet and sometimes brushes his teeth without threats. Why, just a few months ago, he showered voluntarily. Not only that, he's very smart and has tons and tons of interests, ranging all the way from *Call of Duty: Black Ops* to *Call of Duty: Modern Warfare.*

I first noticed the look of mischief/love in Lily's eye a few weeks ago, when she walked through the door after school with the Princess.

"Hiiiiiiii cutie," said Lily, sashaying over to give him a hug.

He didn't return her affections. Didn't even glance up from his iPod. Very busy with crucial *Call of Duty* missions.

"Hi," he mumbled.

The girls giggled and thumped up the stairs.

"I think she likes you!" I told him.

His brows shot up, but he didn't raise his eyes. "I know she does."

So, after that frank expression of undying affection, you can imagine my curiosity when I found texts like these, here on my screen:

Lily: Is this my boyfriend?

Hobo: Yes. ;(

The adoration! It's palpable. He likes her—you can tell by this . . . what is this?

;(

A sad face? A wink? A sa-wink?

Read on, another day, as Lily checks in:

Lily: Hey babe!

Hobo: OK quit I'm going to school bye

Good boy. Education first. But still, unmistakable devotion to his girl, no? In this next excerpted text, he stays true to school—and stuff:

Hobo: OK I'm doing something else

Lily: What?

Hobo: Getting ready for school

Lily: When is your school?

Hobo: Plus I'm playing video games it starts at 9

Lily: You have plenty of time!

Hobo: My bus leaves at 8 I just woke up!

Priorities, Lily! One must have an hour before school to play video games and completely avoid grooming. Everybody knows that.

The tension builds between the lovebirds:

Lily: Did you miss me Tuesday?

Hobo: If it makes you sleep at night

Lily: Haha oh we need to work on you

Hobo: OK I'm doing something else

Well, as you can imagine, sadly—and not unexpectedly—Lily soon tires of the Hobo's inattentiveness, and it all comes to a head. She's had enough.

Lily: We are breaking up!!

Hobo: OK

Lily: We are back together!!

Hobo: Whatever I don't care

Lily: Wow OK

Reunited and it feels so good? I can't tell. What just happened there, and what in the name of SpongeBob SquarePants will happen next?

Will Lily get her Hobo? Will he make it to school on time? Will he *ever* voluntarily take a shower?

We will never know—I don't plan to publish any more texts. The truth is, I questioned whether or not to write about this series. But it was so cute—and relatively harmless. I couldn't resist.

I also checked with Lily's mom first. I wanted to be sure it was all right, because the girl is a doll. Sweet and kind, Lily loves kids—wants to be a pediatrician someday—and she teases my boy with good intentions, because she knows it secretly makes him happy. Deep down, I think he quite enjoys having a beautiful girl flirt with him.

What hobo doesn't enjoy the attentions of a pretty woman?

He's intrigued.

But he's not ready.

I saw it again this past weekend, the lack of "ready," as the Princess and I stopped at Victoria's Secret with the Hobo in tow. He was lost without his iPod to stare at, and he spun around in circles, trying to avoid looking at anything.

Bras! Ahh! Teddies! Ahhhhh! Thongs! *Ahhhhh!!*

Poor kid. Everywhere he turned—*Ahhhhh!*—and finally, declaring himself "scarred for life," he ran and stuck his head into the safest place he could find—the very corner of the store.

No, he's not ready.

That's fine with me. I'm not ready, either.

That boy. He's hygienically challenged. Can't match his shirt and pants. Incapable of combing his hair.

But he can stay that way, because if it was up to me, he'd be tiny again. The tears, the tantrums, the many, many nights sleeping on the hardwood floor beside his crib—I'd take it, I'd do it all again. I'd scoop him up, inhale him and keep him small, keep him with me.

Diapers, tears, tantrums and all.

I try, but I can't stop time. There he is, a fast-growing little guy facing—quite unwillingly—the wall between boy and man. The texts and shopping trips prove it, and they make me laugh.

And sometimes I laugh to keep from crying.

But, no. I won't read or publish anymore of the kids' texts.

Unless they end up on this phone . . .

;(

Sa-wink!

CHAPTER SIX
Showering with Superman Is Not as Much Fun as It Sounds
Saturday, 8:22 a.m.

Shots fired in the basement.

Clearly, the boy's awake.

My son, the Hobo: perpetually dressed like a miniature homeless man. He's a shooter of plastic guns, a maker of messes, an avoider of chores, a producer of odors, an avid fan of farts and a stranger to personal hygiene. Able to fashion a weapon from just about anything—a stick, a shoe, an unfortunate stuffed animal.

The electronic gunfire downstairs tells me that he's playing video games already, before eating breakfast, before getting dressed, probably before opening his eyes. The only thing he does prior to answering the *Call of Duty* is answer the call of nature.

Which reminds me—I have to go. So I stretch, roll out of bed, walk to the bathroom, sit down and . . .

Plop

I'm in the toilet bowl. Thanks a lot, Hobo.

Sometimes I forget I'm the mother of a boy. Life has a way of reminding me—repeatedly.

I dry myself off and head to the kitchen for coffee. I want coffee, anyway, but there are no clean mugs. They're all in the dishwasher—the dishwasher that the boy is supposed to run and empty. In true hobo fashion, he's shrugged off his chores again, and I have to wash out a mug before I can even start the coffeemaker.

After what feels like several millenniums later, I have caffeine and smartphone here in-hand, ready for a little writing. I turn to the kitchen table, where I see that I have company: a rock—on the kitchen table. It's been here, this rock on the table, all through the week, since last Sunday, when the boy placed it here after carrying it in from outside, showing it to all of us, and examining it from all sides while eating dinner. Then, he dubbed it his pet rock.

I start to wonder why no-one-bothered-to-pitch-it-back-out-the-door-but-then-why-do-I-even-ponder-such-things-since-I'm-the-mom-and-it's-my-job. Apparently.

I sigh, and sit down hard—on a gun.

Thanks a lot, Hobo.

There's a gun on the chair, a plastic Nerf gun, a gun that makes a hell of a lot of noise and is now lodged sideways in my lady regions.

Yes, life has many ways of letting me know that I have a son, such as the fact that I sit on guns, dine with rocks and fall into toilets. I also shower with Superman, Spiderman and occasionally, a Camaro.

And speaking of showers—hmmm. I walk to the basement door and yell down the stairs:

"Son. When was the last time you took a bath?"

TV: *Bang-bang-bang-bang-pow!*

Son: *Crickets*

Me: "Son! When was the last time you bathed?!"

Son: "Umm . . . I went swimming Tuesday!"

Face? Meet palm.

Me: "It's Saturday. And I'm not asking about swimming. I'm talking *soap!* I'm talking *shampoo!* I'm talking *washcloth* in your *butt-crack!*"

TV: *Bang-bang-bang-bang-pow!*

Son: *More crickets*

Me: "*Get in the tub! Now!*"

Son: *Streaks up the stairs into bathroom*

Obviously, he could use some hygienic guidance. I follow him in, run water and pour bubble bath as he finishes pulling off his clothes. I catch the unmistakable scent of boy—of dirt, of socks, of Doritos.

Cool Ranch? Nacho Cheese? Probably both.

I glance at the clock: 8:15 a.m. "Have you been eating Doritos already?" I ask.

He pauses, mid-climb, into the tub. But he doesn't look at me. "Well, that was breakfast . . . "

"Doritos aren't breakfast, son. Doritos are nasty . . . MSG . . . Doritos are Doritos."

He says nothing—wisely—and descends into the warm water, fishing around for Superman, Spiderman and the Camaro. I hand him a soapy washcloth and reiterate its many benefits and uses. Then, I return to the kitchen and sit back down to my phone and coffee, his rock and Nerf gun.

As I sip, I remember: It wasn't always like this. Long ago, I had only one child—a little girl—altogether clean, pretty and Dorito-free.

My daughter, age 5, was excited about the birth of her baby brother, figuring that he'd serve as a sweet little live doll that she could dress up and carry around. Knowing this, I recall being very pregnant with my son and taking the Princess to a garage sale that had advertised "tons of infant boys' clothes!" We drove through a rather nice neighborhood to the address, and pulled into an immaculate-looking residence.

Eight months along, I struggled out of the car, and helped my clean, shiny and freshly bathed daughter from her car seat. I waddled into the pristine garage and began scooping up adorable blue onesies from a table as my girl, chattering excitedly, bolted to a different section of the sale, on a mission for doll-brother toys and accessories.

Suddenly, the chatter stopped. Silence was—and is—a rare, almost non-existent concept for the Princess, so I turned to see if she had slipped away or been abducted.

It wasn't a particularly large area, and I quickly spotted her, standing across the room and staring at something. Her mouth had fallen wide open. She stood stock-still. She was, for once, completely speechless. Something was very wrong.

I rushed to her side. "Honey—what is it?"

She shook her head, eyes wide open, jaw still dropped. After what seemed like hours, she spoke.

"Oh, Mommy . . . "

I followed her gaze across the room. There, in a grimy brown oil spill on an otherwise spotless floor, sat a small, filthy creature—a troll? A hobbit?—of some sort, finger-painting in the oil with one hand and shoving Doritos into his mouth with the other.

Cool Ranch? Nacho Cheese? Probably both.

The only giveaway to this grimy thing's species was the dirt-covered diaper on its behind. I joined my daughter, gaping in open-mouthed horror.

"Can't keep him clean."

The woman's voice startled me back into reality. She was behind me: the little troll's mother.

"Can't keep him out of the Doritos, either," she said.

"Oh, well, I . . . " I stuttered around, embarrassed that she'd caught me gawking at her grubby monkey.

She glanced down at the pile of newborn blue onesies in my arms—onesies that had once belonged to her little creature—and then at my bulging belly. "The one on the way. It's your first boy."

This was posed as a statement, not a question.

I nodded slowly, still in shock. But the woman had already turned and walked away, smirking. She didn't say another word.

She didn't have to.
There was no need.

CHAPTER SEVEN
Love Stinks. At Least, Ours Does
Sunday, 5:19 a.m.

The first time.

You meet someone special, you fall in love and it's only natural: You start thinking about it.

You wait for it to happen; you wonder how it will affect your relationship, and you worry how it will be for your new significant other—whether it will pull you closer as a couple, or drive your lover away. Will it be strong and powerful—like an earthquake? Or soft and quiet—like a whisper?

I speak not of the first kiss. I speak not of the first sexual encounter.

I speak, of course, of the first fart.

When I started dating the husband in the spring of 1993, his near perfection amazed me: Here was an extremely handsome man who also seemed extremely kind. In my experience of men at age 24, handsome and kind did not usually go together; a man was either handsome OR kind. Not both.

Never both.

But this new guy astonished me with his sweet, funny, easy-going personality, and his dark, great-looking features. Better still, he was head over heels for me. He told me all the time that I was sexy and beautiful, and though this made me worry about his vision, I soon fell hard for him, too.

There was only one problem. I didn't tell anyone about it. I kept it to myself.

"*Nice guy*," I thought. "*But his car sure smells like farts.*"

I could not understand this. He did not blow any barn-burners in front of me. No, in those first few happy weeks, he didn't emit a single gas from either end. I didn't either of course, for I was a pretty flower who never did such things.

Yet every time I got into his vehicle, I smelled it without fail, and it wasn't me (See comment re: pretty flower, above). The brown, rancid odor was unmistakable, its meaning very clear:

Someone had a heinie hiccup.

Someone took their colon bowlin'.

Someone fucking farted.

But I was young and newly in love and I never said anything to him about the methane monsters lurking in his Ford. Instead, I told myself that it must have been the used car's previous owner who had the booty bomb problem, because my guy was flawless. Burping, farting, ball-scratching, etc. were the stuff of mere mortals, of cretins.

Over the course of a few weeks, er, months, in the way these things go, one night we got biblical with each other. We had our hands and what-nots all over each other's swimsuit areas for a good, sweaty 30 minutes; an impressive amount of time, I know, but remember—we were in our 20s. We finished our, um, Bible study and fell asleep blissfully, nested like spoons.

And that's when it happened.

Bwarrrppppppp!

My eyes popped wide open. I lay there in the dark, frozen, not believing what I had heard. Surely, I'd been dreaming. Surely, it couldn't be what I thought.

But, lo—there was a sequel.

Fwweeeerrrrppppp!!!

Ahh! My thighs, my thighs! Realizing my legs and stomach were spooned against an active bung blower, I launched back from his body like a slingshot and scooted as far away from him as possible, to the very edge of the bed.

"Sorry," he whispered, still half asleep but embarrassed and awakened by his own blanket bomb.

I'd like to say he never farted again after this incident. I'd like to say that, but it would be a lie. He just couldn't seem to stop himself anymore. He'd broken the seal; he'd blown the volcano; he'd popped his cherry.

Flearrrppp!

He blasted at breakfast.

Thuurrrrppppp!

He blew at lunch.

Bwarrrppppp!

He back-drafted at dinner.

He tush-tickled on the sidewalk; he cheesed them at the store. He rump-ripped in the movie theater, and then he did it more.

And always, always, always—he farted in his car.

"Well. That explains a lot," I said, as we drove down the road one day after a particularly loud bratwurst bugle.

"Huh? What do you mean?" he asked. His emissions had apparently become white noise for him—he couldn't even hear them anymore.

"Your car," I said. "It stinks—smells like farts. I noticed it when you picked me up for our first date."

He nodded. "That's because I farted all the way from my apartment to yours, then I farted all the way home after we went out," he looked over at me sheepishly. "I was trying to get rid of them when you weren't around."

"That's really . . . considerate," I said. "So how come you feel you can do it in front of me now? Like, all the time? And everywhere?"

"Well, it hurts to hold it in," he replied, aiming puppy-dog brown eyes at me. "And since you know what I'm really like now, I was hoping you'd love me anyway."

I said nothing and rolled down the window. I tried to focus, but the fumes had made my eyes water.

"You look really pretty today!" he offered.

I stared out the open window, gulping great mouthfuls of oxygen, and wondered if I could do it. Now that I knew his secret, could I put up with his constant noxious emissions for the long haul? Could I deal with his turtle-burps, his mud-slappers, his crack-rattlers?

Yeah. That was 20 years ago. Twenty years, two kids, one mortgage, three dogs, five cats, nine cars and 10,984,367 farts ago.

And over these last couple of decades, I've learned a few things. As much as I hate to admit it, he was right: It does hurt to hold it in. I have also learned to, um, "give" as well as receive the aromatic gifts he bestows so generously unto me. I cannot begin to approach his level of expertise in this area, but I have to say—I can deal them. I am middle-aged, growing ever older, and much to my great dismay, I am human.

I am no longer a pretty flower.

You know what, though? He loves me anyway. He's such a nice guy.

But—wow. His car sure smells like farts.

CHAPTER EIGHT
Birthday Party in Three Hours. Me: Urgent!
Husband: Couch
Saturday, 10:44 a.m.

Well, it's my son's eleventh birthday, and out here in the country, you know what that means:

I had to buy a bunch of guns.

Nerf guns, that is, as well as Nerf bullets, for the Hobo and all his friends. Because nothing says "Happy Birthday!" like a mass shooting. With hundreds of foam darts.

I know what little redneck boys like: violence. I was a little redneck boy myself once—a tomboy, anyway. I spent a good bit of the 1970s tussling and wrestling with my childhood friend, Marshall the Neighbor Boy, who remained blissfully unaware of the fact that I was actually a girl, though I didn't help him any, as I dressed like a miniature lumberjack.

But back to the Hobo: What his birthday *really* means is that I'm throwing him yet another party, approximately his 37th, or so it seems.

I'm not—what is it the kids say?—"down with" this modern trend of throwing my children a giant birthday event, complete with inflatables and clowns, rainbows and unicorns, every single year. In my entire 17-odd years of childhood, I remember exactly one (1) birthday party, wherein a few friends came over for about two hours, and our sole entertainment was a rousing game of Run Around Granddad's Pool Table. As I recall, I received at this event a Barbie doll, an out-of-the-box Duncan Hines sheet-cake, and a scorching case of chickenpox from one of the guests.

I shared the story of my one (1) childhood soiree with the boy after he requested his eleventh (11th) birthday party, and asked him at what age, did he think, we could stop throwing huge parties for him?

"Um . . . 12?"

(And last year's answer was "Um . . . 11?")

But he's growing up fast—and so is his sister. She turned 16 last May, and I threw her a Sweet 16 party, which will probably be the final bash of her childhood—amazing, since her first birthday was, like, yesterday.

So, yes. Though I'm not a proponent of Ridiculous Rainbow Unicorn Parties for the kiddies, time and mommy guilt still drive me to throw them a pretty good shindig most years. This year was no different: I set a date, printed up invites, purchased appetizers and pop and ordered a cake. I researched games, collected RSVPs, and most importantly—I bought weapons.

Although I plan and shop (and plan and shop some more) far in advance for these things, I still manage to stress way the hell out on the actual Saturday of the soiree. The day-of tasks get me every time, and so this morning, I find myself in the usual pre-party frenzy.

The husband fails to see any urgency in the situation—completely understandable, of course, as there is a college football game on television.

There is *always* a college football game on television.

While I scurry around, making food and scrubbing toilets, the husband sprawls on the couch, eating Doritos, watching the game and scratching himself.

I pause from preparations long enough to glare and sigh repeatedly at him, and then notice that the sofa cushions underneath him are covered in dog hair. I dig out the pet-hair remover roller, and hopefully—some would say naively—place it beside him on the couch, thinking my husband will see it and give me a little assistance.

Did you see what I did there? I said "husband" and "assistance" in the same sentence.

Those of you familiar with the male of the species can predict what happens with the roller and the fur-covered couch—nothing. As I frown and cuss under my breath, well, that's when it hits me:

I should plan like a man.

As I said, I commit weeks, months, entire slabs of company time to putting together parties for the kids. Guest lists are drafted, themes are considered, invitations are made and favors are purchased, resulting in a huge Disney-sponsored event complete with matching plates, napkins and goodie bags.

The husband commits . . . to watching the OSU/Florida A&M game.

Honestly, maybe he's got something there. Maybe the Man Plan would be the way to go for the kids' birthdays. I could just pick up some pop, a little cake and maybe a bag of Doritos and toss them on the table. Then, I'd plop on the couch, turn on the TV and commence scratching myself.

But I can't do that for this year's party—I'm in far too deep. I've already made elaborate plans, purchased ammo, and I really need some help. So with Clorox wipes in one hand, Nerf guns in the other, I walk across the room to where the husband lounges on the couch, atop the dog dander.

"You may not be aware of this," I tell him, "but we're having Levi's birthday party today."

"Huh," he grunts, eyes on the TV.

"Could you help me get ready?"

"Huh," he says still transfixed.

Hmm. I wonder . . .

"Do you want to go in the bedroom and have steamy-hot monkey-sex with me?"

"Huh," he mumbles, shoveling a handful of Doritos into his mouth.

"Huh" indeed. Call it genius, call it psychic, call it women's intuition, but right here, I know that:

1) He is not listening to me; and

2) It's a good thing my Nerf guns aren't real guns.

You see, I regard September 20th as a momentous occasion, a blessed event, the Day of Our Son's Birth.

My husband regards September 20th as—September 20th.

Oh. And the day of the OSU/Florida A & M game.

CHAPTER NINE
It's Mother's Day. There Will Be No Complaining
Sunday, 9:56 a.m.

I have two wishes. I can't even think of a third.

It's Mother's Day, and all I really want is:

1) Outdoor time with the family; and

2) A microwave bacon tray.

Yeah, I admit it. Lately, I've been struggling with bacon. Show me a decent recipe, and I can cook just about anything. Fancy cakes and cookies, large Thanksgiving dinners—give me a glass or three of wine, and I have the patience and know-how to make sushi.

But for some reason, I lack the remedial skills required to fry bacon. I've tried all the methods, the new, the old, the Google: Bacon in a skillet—a mess. Bacon in the oven—a mess. Bacon on the grill—a mess, a fire and a damn good thing I bought an extinguisher.

The kids love bacon; they ask for it every weekend. So when I heard about the microwave tray, I was all over it, as I am a huge fan of ridiculous, space-hogging kitchen gadgets that may or may not work.

The husband made Mother's Day Wish Two come true with $12.99 and a quick trip to Walmart, and I nuked up some bacon with the new tray.

There was no mess. There was no fire. It was a big ol' bacon success.

As I sit here staring out the kitchen window, I realize that my other wish—family time in the great outdoors—will prove far more difficult to achieve. The kids would much rather stay inside and stare passively at computer/iPhone/video game screens than engage in any sort of interaction with actual humans. Even on the most beautiful of days, they sit frozen in a screen stupor, clicking and tapping their lives away.

Of course, this drives me crazy, and every so often I suggest to them, in a calm, rational fashion, that they should go outside:

"It's gorgeous today, Hobo. How about you turn off *Call of Duty* and we throw the ball?"

"Look, Princess, how nice it is out there! Why don't you put down your iPhone and sit in the sun with me?"

"Oh my *God*, you two! Don't you realize that you will spend your *entire adult lives* in front of a computer screen at work? Turn that crap off and go *outside* while you still can! *Now-uhh*!"

So, yes. I just want to spend time with my family in the fresh air and sunshine, and I decide to accomplish this by asking/coercing/demanding that everyone go fishing with me—without complaint.

"*Let's go fishing*," I think.

"*It'll be fun*," I think.

A daunting goal, the "no complaints" part of the equation, but it is one I feel I can accomplish with bacon, cookies and guilt. Lots and lots of guilt.

The weather looks decent today; somewhat chilly, but sunny, pleasant and overall, not bad. Do I check the forecast? I do not.

It's Ohio. Forecasts don't matter—weather subject to change.

I load the car. I pack chairs, lunch and fishing gear; I pack bacon, cookies and guilt.

Then I approach the kids, who are engrossed, as always, in clicking and tapping.

"Let's go fishing!" I say.

Clickety-tap

"It will be fun!" I say.

Tappity-click

"I made bacon!"

They glance up.

"Aw! Why can't we just eat it here?" asks the Hobo.

"No way. I packed a picnic, and we'll all be outside and there will be *no gadgets* and *absolutely no complaining* because it's Mother's Day."

"But . . . " chirps the Princess.

"I said no complaining! It's *Mother's Day*!"

They shuffle to the car, looking defeated and compliant, just the way I like them. The husband starts the engine, and the sky turns dark—of course it does. And as we pull onto the main road, the wind picks up. As we arrive at the park, the leaves flip backwards. As we walk to the lake, a dark blue curtain of rain forms to the west.

Of course it does.

"Great day for fishing!" says the husband.

I spin my head around. "It will be fun," I hiss. "No complaining. It's *Mother's Day*!"

We arrive at the dock as the first drops fall. The kids and I put down our supplies and chairs while the husband untangles the rods and opens the tub of bait.

"Whoa! What happened to these worms?" he says, recoiling.

"Well, I put some water in there," I reply. "They looked a little dry."

He raises his eyebrows. "They're wet now, all right. It's worm soup in here. Most of them are dead."

We bait our hooks with what's left, and the children listlessly cast their lines. Pouring rain, icy wind, dead worms: It's plainly time for lunch.

"Who's ready to eat? I packed bacon!"

Both kids look down at their muddy, worm-flesh-encrusted fingernails.

"Um, no. Thanks," mumbles the girl.

"Not me!" says the boy.

I plop down in my chair, cast my line and think about the good old days, when they spent their time begging me to play outside with them.

"*Mommy! Play catch with me!*"

"*Take me to the park!*"

"*Let's jump on the trampoline!*"

These requests always occurred at convenient moments, such as job interviews, annual mammograms and bowel movements.

They're busy now, growing up, and rarely want me to accompany them outdoors. The truth is that I miss them—and they're not even gone. Yet.

As I sit thinking these happy and uplifting thoughts, the rain picks up and the wind blows icy lake water onto the dock. The boy shivers; the girl shakes. But they do not complain.

For 20 minutes.

"Mom. I am *so cold*," says the Princess, hunched over in her chair.

The Hobo throws down his pole and sprawls in the middle of the dock, his face soaked from rain. "Ughhhh," he moans.

I glance from the kids to the clouds to the rain; to the wet, wind-bent trees to the tub of dead worms.

"*Let's go fishing,*" I'd said.

"*It will be fun,*" I'd said.

I turn to the husband. "Come on. Let's go."

"Are you sure?" he says. "Because I know you wanted to be outside, and it's Mother's Day . . . "

I rise from my seat. "Oh, I'm sure."

We pack up the chairs and all the gear. The kids shuffle ahead of us back to the car, looking defeated and compliant.

Just the way I like them.

And we head home—to soap, to towels, to warmth, to video games and iPhones and computers.

It certainly turned out to be a cold, crappy Mother's Day. But as we pull into the driveway, I get an idea:

"*Let's play a board game,*" I think.

"*It'll be fun!*" I think.

Yet another daunting goal, persuading two screen-addicted kids to play an actual physical board game.

But I know I can get my way, using bacon, cookies and guilt. Lots and lots of guilt.

CHAPTER TEN
He's Rolling the Stones. Yes, That Is a Euphemism for Something
Tuesday, 9:11 p.m.

I suppose it's nice that my husband has something to keep him busy in his spare time—something that holds his interest, occupies his hands, something that makes him happy. Hey—I can't always be around to entertain him.

He really enjoys it, too. I can tell. He does it first thing every morning, in the afternoon and all throughout the evening. He does it in the kitchen, the living room, and I have no doubt he does it in his cubicle at work. I have even seen him trying to do it in his sleep.

I'm not talking about hunting or fishing, coin-collecting or guitar-playing. I'm not talking about football or cars or woodworking. I'm talking about good, old-fashioned, apple-pie-American . . .

. . . ball-scratching.

I became aware of his pastime early in our marriage, after accidentally walking into the crime scene on several occasions. Because we were newlyweds, it took me a while to muster the courage to ask about it, until one day, when I found him in the living room watching football and busily digging in his coin purse—again.

"You finding anything good in there?"

"Huh?" he replied, completely unaware, apparently, that he was knocking his knackers.

I motioned to the crime at hand. "You scratch. Your balls. All the time."

"Yeah, well, they itch."

"Do you have some kind of medical condition that I should have been made aware of?" I said, cocking my head. "Like, before we got married?"

"No, no—I'm clean," he said. "They just itch sometimes, that's all."

Disgusted, I left the room and went into the kitchen to load the dishwasher, where he joined me a few minutes later. Still scratching his scallops, he walked to the refrigerator, pulled his hands from his shorts and yanked open the door.

Aahhhhhh!

The germs, the *germs* my beloved had just deposited on the container we used to hold our food. Our *food!*

I covered my face, hoping to erase the mental picture of what I'd just witnessed, but it was no use. My mind's eye could still picture the millions of bacteria now writhing on the fridge handle.

When I finally dared to look again, he'd pulled out a two-liter of Diet Coke and made his way to the kitchen cupboard, one hand on the bottle, the other going down again for a quick junk jangle before reaching in for a glass. He poured some pop, took a sip, paused thoughtfully for a minute, and headed back to the refrigerator for . . .

. . . For what? Where would he spread his DNA of doom next?

The ice. The ice! My God, the *ice!*

"Nooooooo!" I yelled, throwing myself in front of the freezer door.

He stared at me, wide-eyed and alarmed. "What is wrong with you?!"

"Your hands!" I said. "You're touching *everything!* After you scratched your balls!"

"Yeah, well—hands touch things. That's what they do."

"OK, but do you have to touch the fridge and the pop and the glasses and *the ice?!*"

"If I want a cold drink, I have to—yes!" he said, visibly annoyed.

I opened the door and reached into the bin. "Here—let me get it for you," I said, dumping some cubes into his glass. "I have never, in all my life, seen so much ball-scratching."

"Give me a break, would you? It's the weekend; I haven't showered yet today." He turned and headed back to the living room and the TV. "They just itch sometimes, that's all."

I pondered this information, hoping it was just a passing phase. He hadn't crackered his jacks at all *before* we got married.

Ah, but over the next few months, I met the real man. And I soon found out his berry-picking was only the beginning. He had dozens of disturbing "manly" habits including—but not limited to—pooping with the bathroom door open; sneezing without covering his mouth; and, as I've mentioned, releasing gases anytime, anywhere and from either end. It rained bodily fluids constantly at our place. And not in any kind of newlywed way.

For a woman like me who had only lived with other females, these were all-new, unhygienic and truly frightening practices. They alarmed me. And, I admit it. I went a little crazy.

I changed. I morphed. I transformed. I became . . . Bacteria Banshee.

Able to leap for Clorox wipes in a single bound! More powerful than any super-virus! Look! There with the hand sanitizer! It's a maid! It's Mrs. Clean! No—it's Bacteria Banshee!

Watch as Bacteria Banshee reaches the ice bin before her spouse! Marvel at her ability to lunge for the disinfectant can! Listen as she provides helpful public service announcements!

"Use a *&$%# tissue!"

"Wash your ^&*# -ing hands!"

"For f*#x sake, shut the bathroom door when you poop!"

Wacky new commands like these perplexed my mate—at first.

But I sprayed, wiped and cajoled; I slammed, washed and bitched. And, for the most part, over these 20 years, he's learned to do what I asked—lest he suffer Bacteria Banshee's Lysol wrath.

"Yes, dear," is his mantra.

Except when it comes to ball-scratching. True, I have made some antimicrobial progress with my man, but try as I might, I cannot keep him from rolling the stones. His dedication to this task continues to amaze me; truly, he's elevated scrotum-scraping to a high art form. There is not a week, a day, barely an hour that goes by that I don't catch him minding the twins.

"They just itch sometimes, that's all," is his other mantra.

No, I can't seem to stop the jingling of the bells.

Nonetheless, I remain hard at work, raising antibacterial awareness everywhere—except my husband's shorts. Because we all know that when germs are left unchecked, bad things happen in this country, such as pandemics and swine flus and George Bushes.

And though I can't keep him from bobbing his apples, I will not give up. I am Clorox-wiping. I am sanitizer-toting. I am Bacteria Banshee.

Hey. He has his hobbies, I have mine.

CHAPTER ELEVEN
The Family That Raps Together Stays Together
Wednesday, 6:17 p.m.

I have been strongly encouraged not to sing. Ever.

I'm not sure why. I'm a great singer. Just ask me—I'll tell you.

"I'm a great singer!" I'll say.

Who do I sound like, you ask? Carrie Underwood? Katy Perry? Lady Gaga, maybe?

Nope. Someone more famous, more legendary than any of those ladies. My voice has been compared to that of the incomparable, the irrepressible, the unforgettable . . .

. . . Neil Young.

I know, I know—all of y'all have turned green with musical envy. And I understand. I do. Because, really—why sing like a soft, pretty woman when you can croon like a caterwauling hillbilly?

Most folks don't say anything when I sing, no doubt struck speechless by my incredible vocal skills. My daughter's the only one who says she doesn't want to hear me.

I'm not sure why. Wasn't that long ago, I bought her a little blue karaoke machine and we sat on her bedroom carpet belting out Sheryl Crow. Eventually I bought her another microphone for the machine, and we sang songs together.

"You're a really good singer, Mommy," she said.

Such a sweet little Neil Young fan.

I don't know what happened. Now she rolls her eyes and inserts earbuds at my slightest hum. And I am not to sing ever in front of her friends.

But today, I'm following the rules, sitting here in the SUV with the Princess and her crew while we wait for cheer practice to start. I've got my head down, writing on my phone and keeping my mouth shut, trying not to do anything embarrassing for her. Such as breathing.

She plugs her phone into the car stereo and begins playing music from people with first names like "Lil" and last names like "Thug."

I will myself deaf.

Although she's not allowed to listen to music with lots of bad words, I still hear shreds of phrases that gray my hair. Words that rhyme with "sick" and "duck." Words she shouldn't understand yet. Or ever.

It's a losing battle, because as she always says:

"Mom, I ride the school bus. I know things."

Kill me now.

In fact, she knows everything. Just ask her. And I don't know anything these days. Just ask her.

I certainly don't want to learn the lyrics to any of her music; I'm just able to grasp words here and there. The ones that rhyme with "duck" and "sick." After a few minutes of listening to Lil Thug, I feel the need to shower, go to confession—maybe get a prescription for antibiotics.

But in the interest of peace, I shut my mouth, put it all out of my mind and try to concentrate on writing. My brain goes to its happy place, separating itself from the sounds of Lil Thug, and my inner jukebox plays some mellow 70s soft rock. Something long ago made into Muzak. Something smacking of daisies and white gauzy dresses and orange-balled sunsets.

What? Have you never been mellow?

Smack-dab in the middle of my silent Olivia Newton-John reverie, I almost don't notice when Lil Thug abruptly stops, and the girl cues up something different. Something kind of . . . awesome.

"I like big butts . . ."

My hips start wiggling, head begins bobbing of its own accord. Could it be? Yes, yes—she's playing *Baby Got Back*, by Sir Mix-A-Lot, circa 1992, and she's enjoying it too. From the corner of my eye I see the smile, the head-bob so much like mine.

But I dare not sing. No sir. I know my role: the Silent Chauffeur. It's very hard to contain myself, but I don't want to humiliate her. I have to stay content with covert wiggling.

I look in my rearview mirror at the girls in the back seat. They're loving this 20-plus-year-old song, all three bouncing, dancing, singing. My daughter cranks the volume to speaker-blowing levels, and I bite my tongue as the Honda thumps like a pimped-out Detroit Caddy.

And that's when, all of a sudden, it happens. The unthinkable. The unbelievable.

"Sing it, Mom! C'mon! You know every word!" says my daughter, excitement in her voice.

Glancing over in the passenger seat, I wonder: Who is this child? Am I in the right car? Am I dreaming? Am I high?

I can't quite believe my luck. Not only unbanned from singing, I'm encouraged to sing. This hadn't happened in years.

And she is right. Bad-ass gangsta that I am, I've memorized every word to the song. I knew it would be a valuable skill someday.

As I rap, it strikes me that the song has some of what they call teachable moments: Mr. Mix-A-Lot makes it very clear that he appreciates a, um, round female form, girls who "pack back" and eat red beans and rice. I hope the girls in my vehicle are catching this. Apparently sexy women eat food.

Though chock-full of sage wisdom, Mr. Mix is no saint, as evidenced by some of the song's words. And I'm not sure whether to sing one particular line, a sentence with questionable imagery in which he compares a part of his anatomy to that of an anaconda.

Then I remember: They listen to Lil Thug. They ride the school bus. They know things.

Kill me now.

So I do it. Loud and proud, I belt out the line where the singer's snake doesn't want none . . .

". . . unless you got buns, hon!"

Laughter, smiles and giggles erupt, all around. From girls. From teenagers.

From my daughter.

Well. Hell hath surely frozen over in the Honda.

I made the right decision, throwing down that lyric. Maybe not a "teachable moment." But a "moment" nonetheless.

Thank you, Sir Mix-A-Lot.

CHAPTER TWELVE
The Princess Got Her Driver's Permit. Pray for Me
Friday, 7:39 p.m.

Pull over, people. Here she comes.

Good grief, how did it happen? My daughter, the Princess, is driving the Honda. She's cresting a hill, white-knuckled, bespectacled, 15-and-a-half. Just received her driver's permit.

Pray for me.

Here beside her in the passenger seat, I decide it's high time I give her some valuable advice. I do this often. Is she awake? Is she walking? Is she breathing? I should definitely offer her my guidance on these activities.

"Now, when you're on these back roads like this . . ."

"I know. I know what you're going to say, Mom—watch out for the deer."

She knows, she says.

I see her eye-roll, but it doesn't stop me. No sir.

"Well, it's not just the deer, you gotta . . ."

"I know, Mom. You told me. Watch out for the Amish."

"Yeah, you have to watch out for the buggies, but . . ."

"I know, Mom, go slow."

"Go slow, but what I'm *trying* to tell you is to stay in your lane and watch out for the other people," I turn toward her so she can better absorb my expertise. "A lot of times they will be left of center, especially some of these rednecks. They think the center line is just a suggestion."

"I know, Mom."

She knows, she says.

I roll my eyes, then look back down at my phone to continue writing.

"I am *just saying*. Watch out."

Who said she could have a permit? The State of Ohio? No one consulted *me* on this decision, though I guess I could have said no. It all happened so fast.

I didn't have time.

We just strapped her into the baby seat, like, yesterday, there at the hospital. I didn't trust that contraption—or our clumsy adjustment of its confounding buckles and straps—so I sat in the back with her as the husband drove home. Lord, was I sore.

And terrified.

I wanted to bundle her, from the neck down, in bubble wrap, maybe some packing peanuts. But covering an infant in plastic products of any sort tends to be frowned upon by the authorities.

So I hoisted myself over her body and the hulking baby carrier, and wrapped my arms around the whole thing. As if I could hold it still. As if I could keep her safe.

As if.

She was 7 pounds, 13 ounces, 21 inches long.

Blink

She is 100 pounds, 5 feet, 1 inch.

At her age, I was also 100 pounds and 5 feet, 1 inch. My hobbies included chasing boys, attending parties and depositing my car into the ditch.

I wrecked, in various vehicles, three times before I turned 21, and, though I was no angel, I managed to merrily and obliviously do all this without the assistance of drugs or alcohol. Who knows what would have happened if I'd been driving loaded. But each time, I was stone sober, and lucky to end up alive.

Tell me: What possesses us, as a species, to trust flesh, bone and spirit to 3,000 lbs. of glass and steel? What makes us think we can hurtle our bodies through space at 65 miles per hour and survive if we crash? Sometimes, we don't.

She's so tiny, so fragile—head poking over the wheel, feet barely reaching the pedals. It's very odd, watching your kid drive. It feels exciting and completely idiotic at the same time, like riding bareback on a green-broke horse.

Or letting a child drive a car.

But I want her to have a good time. I want her to go and chase boys and be young, because there is nothing like that time, before adulthood and jobs, when the car's just a rolling jukebox and the streets run only to freedom and friends and fun.

She should enjoy the road while she can. Soon enough, driving will become just a necessary task, hair-raising transportation to work. Every day, in my hour-long interstate commute, I pass serious, sometimes fatal accidents, hundreds of people intent on playing "screw your neighbor" at 80 mph. I've worn years off my life driving with these idiots—my blood pressure, heart rate and pulse spiking for 60 minutes each way, each day. Honestly, I don't know what happens to people at rush hour.

I think about all this as we approach the turn onto Beaver-Springfield Road, and I tell her to slow down. It's wonderful talking to her, here in the car, where she can't escape. It's also good she's with me. Every trip with the husband, her dad—Mr. Swervy McDangerPants—is another terrifying episode of How Not to Drive.

So while I can, I better give her more of my valuable advice: How easy it is to become distracted, to take a curve too fast, to go left of center. How quickly life can spin out of control.

Looking out the window, I keep offering wisdom, feeling satisfied with my ongoing study and critique of her driving skills. Yes, I plan to take every opportunity to further educate her on the art of safe and effective motor vehicle operation.

In fact, I plan to take every opportunity to further educate her on the art of *everything*. It's a generous gesture on my part. But I'm a giver. And she really appreciates it—I can tell.

"I know, Mom, I know. You told me."

She rolls her eyes.

"I am *just saying*. Watch out."

I roll my eyes.

And we head further on down the road.

CHAPTER THIRTEEN
Blood, Flesh and Bone? Nope. Cash, Coins and Credit
Saturday, 6:09 p.m.

I'm worried about the children.

Specifically, I'm concerned about their vision. I really need to get their eyes checked, because when my kids look at me, all they see is money.

And even though they see nothing but dollar signs when they glance my way, they are completely blind to other things, especially their own possessions. Listen, if you will, to a recent conversation with the Hobo:

"Hey Mom," he said. "I need a laptop."

I glanced into the sunroom where, sitting on the desk, was what appeared to be his laptop.

"Um," I pointed to the desk. "Isn't that your laptop right there?"

"Yeah, but I need a *new* laptop."

I cocked my head and tried to remember back to when I'd spent a stack of perfectly good U.S. dollars—several hundred of them, in fact—to buy the computer for him, the one that sat gleaming in the sunlight. It wasn't hard to recall. I'd just bought the thing.

"Son," I said, trying to control my bubbling blood pressure, "I got that laptop for you less than a year ago. What are you talking about?"

"Yeah, but it's not very good. Minecraft runs soooo sloowwww on it."

I took a few deep breaths and closed my eyes, reaching for some patience, since my own notebook computer dates to the last millennium, and, I might add, works just fine.

Although his laptop is new, at least by my standards, I will admit that I may not have purchased a top-of-the-line model for him. No, it may not possess the fastest, most advanced video/graphics card, one that would provide him with the ultimate Minecraft (a.k.a. Minecrack) experience.

40

That's because, since day one, the Hobo has been the absolute kiss of death for any PC he touches. He loves computers.

He murders computers.

Viruses, Trojans, worms, more viruses—at least three systems have fallen victim to his incessant web surfing and gaming. And honestly, I don't feel the boy needs a laptop at all, let alone an expensive one—he's 11 years old. What's he going to do with it, write a campaign speech? End world hunger? Whip up a SpongeBob PowerPoint?

He, however, fails to see it this way. Again—vision problems.

But it's not just the boy who's impaired when it comes to financial matters—my daughter is quite challenged, too, judging by this scene a few months earlier:

"Hey Mom," she said. "This weekend? Can I get a manicure?"

I glanced up at her from the laundry pile I was buried in/sorting through, and thought back to the last—and only—time I had a manicure. Again, it involved a different millennium. I know damn sure I paid for it myself.

So I asked her, "Got any money?"

Hands flew to little teenage hips, and her mouth dropped open.

"What? I thought you'd pay for it!" she shouted. Oh yes—I call her The Princess for a reason. "I thought we could both go get one!"

Has she met me? Surely she's mistaken me for someone else. My hands are useful, not ornamental, and though I wash them 700 times a day, I'm lucky if my nails look clean. Earlier that morning, I'd stood over the toilet bowl and chopped them off the way I do every couple of weeks.

A nail clip and 45 seconds bent over a commode: That's my manicure.

"Again, I say, you got any money?"

She turned on her heel and stomped to her room. I stayed in my mountain of laundry, and my mind traveled back to my own childhood, when all I wanted was a 64-pack of Crayolas—with built-in sharpener.

And so my mom bought me the 48-pack of Crayolas—with no built-in sharpener—every time.

"Mom," I asked her (over and over again), "Could I get the 64-pack? With the built-in sharpener?"

"You got any money?"

I did not. Forty-eight crayons for me.

"When I was your age," she said (over and over again), "I got *eight* crayons—that's it. I was lucky to have those."

I turned on my heel and stomped to my room. My mother, no doubt, stayed in her mountain of laundry.

That's the way it goes, I guess. Every American generation gets more— much more—than the one before it. And every American generation asks for more—*much* more—than the one before it.

Of course, it's not that way for everyone. I recently watched a documentary about education in third-world countries. The young students, squatted in a "classroom" on a filthy dirt floor (this was a newer film, mind you, not the Great Depression) writing their lessons on broken slabs of slates with rocks. Not a laptop, not crayons—slate.

And rocks.

I think of those children tonight, as we sit at Ruby Tuesday and the waitress gives us two brand-new crayons with the kids' menus. Crayons that will be thrown away at the end of the meal, along with all the leftover food.

"You guys," I say, picking up a perfect red Crayola and waving it in front of both of my son and daughter, "I saw this show on TV the other day, and some of the kids in poor countries don't even have crayons."

The Hobo colors; the Princess taps her iPhone. Do they not see me? Again—vision issues, maybe hearing problems, perhaps ADD. I really should get them to the doctor.

"They have to use broken pieces of slate and rocks to write with," I add.

Scribble-scribble

Tap-tap

"Rocks!" I yell. "To write!"

Nothing. I mean, complete and utter silence.

I give up and watch the waitress fill our water glasses. Since I'm not throwing cash their way, these two are pretty much blind and deaf to me, and not only do they need their eyes checked, they probably could use a thorough hearing screening. Perhaps a complete physical exam.

A full 30 seconds later, the Hobo finally, thankfully speaks up. "Mom?"

I lean his way, to make sure we can hear each other. He looks up from his coloring and deep into my eyes.

That's my boy! I think.

"What is it, buddy?" I ask.

My sweet, sensitive little man. I knew I could count on him.

"I was wondering . . . "

I put my arm around his shoulders, and pull him close to me so we can both remember this Very Teachable Moment. The one sponsored by Crayola and Poor Kids With Rocks.

"When do you think I can get a new laptop?"

Yeah. That boy is going to need medical attention, all right. I withdraw my arm, throw down the crayon and pick up the menu.

All my life, I thought that motherhood really meant something; that the word "mom" stood for values and ideals like support, nurturing and unconditional love.

But right now, I know the truth. Mom just stands for "Made Of Money."

CHAPTER FOURTEEN
The Hobo Made a Decision. Blood Loss Resulted
Tuesday, 3:15 a.m.

Boys are known for many things: dirt, noise, boogers.

Boys are not, however, known for their wise choices.

My son thinks he makes good decisions, but you be the judge, as here are some examples of the decisions he makes on a regular basis:

Doritos: part of this nutritious breakfast.

Showers: just an option.

Pajamas: great for all-day wear.

Oral hygiene: for suckers.

Vegetables: never.

Pizza: forever.

True to boy form, poor choices run rampant in his life, especially since I can't always be around to offer him some of my helpful guidance on what he should and shouldn't do.

In fact, most people could use my guidance on what they should and shouldn't do.

And sure enough, bad decisions are the reason the Hobo ended up in the emergency room at midnight tonight, sniffling and bleeding and needing some stitches.

Let me back up a bit and explain: He's playing football for the first time this year, and we'd picked up his gear today at 10 a.m. At 10:01 a.m., he had the new helmet on his head.

Upon arriving home—still wearing the helmet—my boy hauled his new uniform, pads and equipment bag proudly into the house. He tore off his shirt, and yanked on the chest protector. He couldn't get the stuff on fast enough.

He wore that gear while on the couch; he wore that gear while on the chair. He wore that gear up to his room. He wore that gear most everywhere. (Thank you, Dr. Seuss.)

He proceeded to go about his entire day wearing the helmet, chest protector and little else. He played video games in the helmet. He ate lunch in the helmet. He went to the bathroom in the helmet.

Well, to be clear, he went to the bathroom wearing the helmet, not in the helmet.

As you can tell, the Hobo is pretty stoked for his first football season. I'll admit—it is exciting.

It is also terrifying.

He's 11 years old and solid as a rock, growing like a weed, but many of his classmates have already been playing football for three years. Barely out of diapers, these kids are, when they're thrust to the 50-yard-line.

My son comes from a football family. Both of his paternal uncles played college football; his father lettered in high school football and attended Ohio State University—home of rabid lifelong Buckeye football fans. I'm pretty sure we live near Columbus because of our proximity to OSU. You can imagine my excitement about this.

Up until now, the boy had only a tentative, wary interest in the game. The hitting, the tackling, the potential for injury seemed too much for him. But mostly, games and practice would mean that he couldn't play *Call of Duty* 24/7.

Recently, however, peer pressure wormed its way in—along with a healthy dose of adolescent hormones—and he decided to sign up for football along with most of his friends. Hence, the helmet, which, like I said, he wore everywhere today.

He wore it on the porch, at the table, in his room and the whole time he played video games. Want to know when he didn't wear his helmet?

When he played football.

This evening, he went to a friend's house to spend the night along with another buddy, but he didn't take his new gear, though the boys had big, elaborate plans of practicing. And football practice began in earnest after his friend's parents had gone to bed. Practice began at 10 p.m.

Football practice began in the living room—in front of a stone fireplace.

You see, the boys—the brain trust—decided in their infinite wisdom that the very best location to practice drills and tackles would be in front of a fireplace and hearth built with very large, very solid river rocks.

Tackles. Stone fireplace. 10 p.m. These sound like a series of bad decisions. As you can imagine, at 10:24 p.m., this cell phone rang.

Now, answering the phone after 10 p.m. is never a wise decision; there's no such thing as good news from a call that comes that late. You might as well just slip on your shoes, grab your health insurance card and hop in the car, because a call after 10 means trouble.

A call after 10 p.m. means someone is bleeding. A call after 10 p.m. means someone is hurt. A call after 10 p.m. means someone very likely did something stupid, such as play tackle football without a helmet in front of a large fireplace built with very large, very solid river rocks.

"Hey, guys, everything will be OK, but . . ."

Sure enough, the Hobo was bleeding. The Hobo was hurt. The Hobo did something stupid, such as play tackle football without a helmet in front of a large fireplace. His friend's parents found him dizzy and covered in blood. They cleaned him up and brought him home to us, and he walked in the door at 11 p.m., shaking and dazed.

He was OK, but stitches would be required. I need to be at work early tomorrow—I have a mandatory meeting—and because the wound didn't seem too severe, the husband volunteered to be the one to grab his insurance card, slip on his shoes and drive him to the county hospital in the wee hours of the night. It would be the Hobo's first ER experience, except for the time as a baby, when he screamed bloody murder for two hours and we took him to the hospital where the doctors told us that he just needed to fart. (They were correct.)

But on this trip, after a three-hour wait in ER waiting areas, exam rooms and nurse's stations where staff appeared to be sleeping, my husband said the doctor on duty woke up, took a perfunctory look at my son's head, gave him a numbing shot and quickly—without waiting for the medicine to take effect—grabbed his surgical staple gun.

And before you could say, "He's not numb yet, you asshole!"

Ka-chow-ka-chow-ka-chow!

Our boy got three staple-stitches.

"AHHHH-OWWWWWWW!"

Nobody was asleep in the ER anymore.

The husband just called and told me this tale of medical jack-assery on his way out of the hospital, and that's when I really regretted not going with the guys. The doctor really could have used some of my direction on how to do his job.

Most people could use my direction on how to do their jobs.

I, of course, feel guilty that I didn't go with them. And I might as well have went, because here I am, wide awake, worried and pacing by the window when they arrive home at 3:36 a.m. The boy looks shaken as he stumbles in the door, and he'll have to avoid both wearing a helmet and any more trauma to his head, which is inconvenient, as real, official football practice starts tomorrow.

But despite—or maybe because of—the blood, staples and Dr. Asshole, I think the Hobo learned many lessons tonight, such as the fact that Mom should always be the one go to the ER with him. Not Dad.

Most of all, he learned that there are right and wrong times to wear his football helmet.

But far and away the best time to wear it is when you're actually playing football. Especially in front of a stone fireplace.

CHAPTER FIFTEEN
You Warm Your Bench, I'll Warm Mine
Sunday, 10:07 a.m.

"Son! I washed your girdle and pads for you!"

Huh. That's something I never expected to hear coming out of my mouth. "Girdle," "pads" and "son" are not words I'd think of using in the same sentence, but motherhood has a way of surprising me.

Anyway, you're not a cross-dresser. You're a football player, and girdles and pads are part of your protective gear—important parts, if I want to someday become a grandmother.

I've served as cheer mom, basketball mom and baseball mom, in precisely that order. Now, I am a football mom—an altogether different, rather worrisome affair; one in which I mostly spend my time washing and re-washing the girdle, pads and pants, none of which come clean. Ever.

But they're about as good as they can get for now. So I haul them up the stairs to where you stand, underwear-clad, in the living-room, lanky, gangly—still a hygiene-challenged Hobo—but knocking on the door of adolescence. You begin the process of pulling on the uniform—a 15-minute production that involves wiggling, yanking, sweating and a little bit of luck. This is an awful lot of work, and if it were me, I'd quit. You won't, though.

That's not how you're made.

"I don't want to go to his game!" the Princess yells down from her bedroom. "I have stuff to do!"

She has forgotten, apparently, that you've been watching her cheer for several sports almost every weekend since your birth. You pretty much cut your teeth on bleachers.

"Well, I have stuff to do, too, but I'm going!" I yell back. "He goes to

47

your games! We're a family, and that's what we do for each other. We suffer!"

It's just a typical Sunday at our place, in Beautiful Downtown Brownsville. We don't have spring, summer, fall and winter here, no. We have baseball, basketball and now football season, with a brief one-week respite in mid-summer when we can possibly go on vacation. Maybe. If the coaches say it's OK.

You grab your bag, and rush out the door. "Hurry up, you guys! We're gonna be late!"

Oh yeah—lovely. They've asked us to come to the field an hour-and-a-*half* early, instead of our usual one-hour pre-game routine. We load up, pile in, and after a 40-minute trek down a curvy, hilly road full of Amish buggies, we arrive. You run to your teammates, your sister finds some friends and your dad stakes his spot at the fence.

I climb the steps and park myself alongside several other 30- and 40-something females, my fellow Sheridan Generals Biddy League moms, and—glancing around at all of us—I decide we look pretty good. We definitely do *not* have middle-age spread.

No, we have Bleacher Butt.

Without a doubt, the circumference of our behinds and thighs relate directly to the amount of hours, nay, years our rear-ends and gams have spent on these metal stands. The dimples, the dents on our legs? Not cellulite and not fat. Merely the imprint of seats surely designed by Satan. Modern metal bleachers are uncomfortable, backless, torturous affairs, hotter than the core of the sun in spring/summer, colder than a polar bear pecker now, in late October.

We came as a family to watch you play football. What we mostly do is watch you *not* play football. This is your first year. It shows. And that's OK.

Hey. That bench isn't gonna warm itself.

Secretly, I'm fine with the fact that you don't get much game time. I've never paid much attention to this sport, and now that I'm forced to watch, its raw, visceral nature scares me senseless. You managed to sustain a football-related head injury, requiring stitches, the very first day you received your gear, before the season even started.

So I cringe with each crunch of helmets and shoulder pads. It seems as if we've thrown you to the wolves. It was yesterday—wasn't it?—that I covered you up, strapped you in and kept you safe, in your car seat, the stroller, my arms, even these bleachers. I cannot quite wrap my head around football; around the fact that you're *supposed* to tackle and hit people, that they're *supposed* to tackle and hit you back. Compared to this bloody melee, baseball and basketball are God-dang ballroom dances.

Yes, I'm fine with the fact that you spend most of your time on the sidelines. I see you down there, horsing around with the other benchwarmers while waiting, hopefully, endlessly to get in the game. If I were you, I'd get discouraged; I'd give up.

You won't, though. That's not how you're made.

Sitting here on my bench, watching you on your bench, I think about the things I *should* be doing back home: the laundry piling up, the dishes filling the sink, the dirt scattering across the floor.

And I swear I can feel my Bleacher Butt widening.

I have big plans each week of cooking a healthy, elaborate Sunday dinner. But after a day spent in ice-cold metal stands, all I can manage is a numb-fingered cell-phone dial to the pizza place.

Bah. That's OK.

The dishes will wait. The laundry will still be there. The dirt will remain. And, with luck, the pizza will be ready by the time we pull out of the school parking lot.

Right now, there's nothing I'd rather do than sit here and watch you *not* play football. Hey—these bleachers aren't gonna warm themselves.

Anyway, we're a family, and that's what we do for each other. We suffer.

CHAPTER SIXTEEN
Shopping on Thanksgiving? Oh Hell No
Sunday, 6 a.m.

My children: the lights of my life, the center of my world, and the very reason I pee a little every time I sneeze.

Like most parents, there's very little I won't give my kids. I will offer them all my love, arm-loads of cash, entire weeks full of sleepless nights. The raw physics alone of the fact that I gave birth to them still blows my mind.

Ever pushed a watermelon through a straw? Because I have—twice.

After more than 16 years of motherhood, I'm still in awe of the many and various things I would do for my children; I will do things for them that I would never consider for myself. But of all I would do for them, and all I would give to them, there's one instance where I have to draw the line:

I will not wait in line outside a store to shop—on Thanksgiving.

Oh *hell* no.

It almost came to that this year though, because my son requested a PlayStation 4 for Christmas. A hot new item, I thought it might be difficult to obtain. But I was wrong about that.

It was damn near impossible.

It was complicated and exhausting and required Herculean effort, much like giving birth—only without all the fun and helpful drugs.

The whole thing began last April, when out of nowhere, the Hobo walked up and gave me a hug. "I love you, Mommy," he said, all big brown eyes and bullshit.

Mmm-hmm. Sure you do, son. "What is it you want?"

"I want a Sony PS4!" he exclaimed.

I pointed to the TV. "You already have a PS4. I know because I'm still paying for it."

"No—that's a PS3," he said. "I want a PS4."

"What is the difference between the PS3 and the PS4?" I asked.

"The PS 4 is faster and has better graphics and . . . . "

. . . *Wah-wah-wah, wah-wah-wah-waah.* The Charlie Brown adult voice in my head started up then, and I zoned out. I'd heard this whole spiel at least twice before, when he wanted to upgrade to the PS3, and the PS2 before that. I silently thanked Sony for releasing yet another video game system far more expensive—yet marginally better—than the last one.

" . . . and awesome multi-player capabilities!" He paused, waiting for my enthusiastic response.

"Yeah," I replied, "and how much will this PS4 cost?"

He could barely contain himself, bouncing up and down and smiling, more big brown eyes and bullshit.

"Only between four and five hundred dollars!" he exclaimed. "It's not available yet, but it will be on sale in November. So you can buy it for me for Christmas!"

Well. At least I had six months to save up.

Which I would need: Upon its release on Nov. 16, the Sony PS4 quickly sold out for its $399 MSRP. It was, however, available on Ebay—for $1,100 and up. All other major online sites, Walmart.com, Best Buy.com, Game Stop.com, gave me the same result when I Googled for Sony's newest must-have: "Sold out online. Only available in stores."

After several weeks of fruitless cyber-hunting I decided to begin my "available in stores" search at the local Walmart early one Sunday morning. My heart leapt with joy as I walked up to the electronics checkout and saw an associate ringing up a PS4 for a 50-something woman.

"Excuse me," I asked, pointing to the Sony box. "Do you happen to have any more of those?"

Both women turned and looked at me in a way that was both sympathetic and bemused, as if I were an escaped mental patient. "No, honey. This is the last one of three we received this week," said the cashier. "But we're getting 28 in on Thanksgiving."

Thanksgiving? Was she kidding me? Shopping on Thanksgiving? She really did think I was a mental patient, and apparently, a homeless mental patient: "We'll be setting up a line for it; you'll have to wait in line outside until the store opens," she said.

Walmart. In a Line. Outside. On Thanksgiving.

Oh *hell* no.

I walked away, but not before thanking both women. I am nothing if not a polite homeless mental patient.

Thus began a week's worth of frantic phone calls to the customer service numbers of GameStop, Target, God, etc., and each informed me my call was very important to them, but PS4s were available only in stores. Finding this console was proving about as easy as finding Bin Laden; every sales associate had the same answers:

"The next shipment of PS4s will be for Thanksgiving."

"We're only getting a few . . ."

"You'll probably have to wait!"

"In line!"

"Outside!"

"On Thanksgiving!"

Oh *hell* no.

On the second day of the second week of my search, I finally caught a glimmer of hope on a certain big-box store's website: "Available at the Reynoldsburg store within five days. Order in-store now!"

All that morning at the office, I could barely contain my excitement. Even though I'd have to work overtime to make up for a long lunch—my building was a good 25 minutes from the big-box store's Reynoldsburg location—I knew it'd be worth it. At noon, I clocked out, rushed from the office, walked the six blocks to my car, then raced to the store to order the Hobo's gift.

I was met by a hipster sales rep as soon as I stepped inside. "How can I help you, ma'am?"

Ma'am. Here we go.

"I want to buy a PS4," I said. "Your website stated you'd have them within five days, and I could order one here."

The hipster smirked. "I'm afraid that's not possible, ma'am," he said. He was on thin ice with the m-word. "We're not getting any more in until Thanksgiving."

I flashed my smartphone's screen his way. "But look—your site said I could order one in-store—that it'd be available within five days!"

He squinted at the screen, then smirked and shook his head. "No, I'm afraid that's not right," he said. "We'll get some in on Thanksgiving. You're probably going to have to wait in a line outside, though."

Oh *hell* no.

I thanked Sir Hipster for his help, as well as his extremely accurate website. "No problem!" he said. "Have a great day, ma'am!"

Yeah. Ma'am this, punk.

Later that week on my day off, I drove hopelessly around town, double-checking stores in which I'd previously looked. Everywhere I went, I got the same responses:

"No more until Thanksgiving!"

"You'll have to wait in line!"

"Outside!"

"Before the store opens!"

For the first time ever, it appeared I'd have to disappoint the Hobo on Christmas. I aimed the car towards home, and headed hopelessly down Ohio 79, past Target, Walmart, GameStop, Best Buy . . .

Best Buy. I had already checked with them via phone, and got the same old "Thanksgiving!" spiel, so I hadn't stopped in the store yet. Hmmm. I pulled into the lot, parked, and went inside.

"Can I help you?"

The sales associate was about my age—you know, really young—and refrained from ma'am -ing me. I liked him immediately.

"Hi. I've already called here a few times," I said, "but I thought I'd stop in on the off-chance you have any PS4s today?"

He shook his head. "Nope. Sorry. No more until Thanksgiving. You'll probably . . ."

I finished his sentence. ". . . have to come here on Thanksgiving and wait in a line outside before the store opens. Thanks. That's what I figured." I turned toward the door.

"Wait," he said. "Miss?"

Ooh—"Miss." Like I said, this guy was good. My new BFF. I turned around. "Yes?"

He walked over to me, drawing so near that I could smell his antiperspirant. "You didn't hear this from me. Seriously," he whispered.

"Um, OK?" I said.

He stepped even closer. "There are six PS4s behind the counter. Pre-orders that haven't been picked up. They'll be released Sunday. Not sure what time."

"Great!" I said, fighting the urge to hug him.

"Remember—you didn't hear it from me!"

I nodded, and he turned and disappeared into the cell-phone aisle.

Fast-forward to now, 6 a.m., Sunday morning. My phone alarm rings, and I launch myself from bed to coffee pot to car. I do not pause for showering, hair- or tooth-brushing. When on a mission, common hygiene is not a concern.

I pass only a few cars on my drive to town, steering with one hand and clutching coffee with the other, and though the painfully early hour hurts my soul, I feel optimistic. Surely I'll find a PS4 now. My Best Buy BFF hooked me up. I'll be the first one there!

Except I'm not. Apparently, news of the secret Sonys has spread, and as soon as I pull into the lot, I count eight other cars idling on the asphalt, smoke drifting lazily from warm engines in the cold November air.

I do some quick math—no easy task for a journalism major—but I know enough to calculate the problem. Nine cars minus six PS4s equal one extremely disappointed 11-year-old. I glance at my early-morning disheveled face and hair in the rearview mirror, cussing and pouting and considering a good old-fashioned nervous breakdown. This search is truly making me nuts, and I've just decided to put the car in gear and drive my crazy-looking ass away when I see a blue-shirted employee labeled "manager" approach the door. I roll down the window, painfully aware of my questionable hygiene.

"Yes?

"Mornin', ma'am," he says, already off to a bad start with the m-word. "Are you here for anything special?"

"Well, no," I lie, not wanting to dime out my Best Buy buddy. "No. I'm just waiting for the store to open."

He tilts his head. "Are you *sure* you aren't here for a reason?" he asks.

Crap. Busted. "Well, I was hoping that maybe you'd have a PS4. I was just driving by and . . ."

He smiles and pulls a paper from his pocket. "You're in luck."

"Huh?" I reply, squinting up at him.

"You're looking for a Sony PS4, right?"

I nod.

He hands me the sheet. "Take this into the store when it opens and they'll ring you up," he says. "It's the last one. You got it."

I got it. I got it. Great Sony's ghost—I got it!

That is how one finds oneself, with nuclear-grade coffee breath and unwashed bed-head, leaping from a car on a Sunday morning to hug an extremely alarmed Best Buy manager. Even though he called her ma'am. Although the whole thing was difficult . . . and a pain . . . and an epic adventure in four or five parts, it will be, of course, all worth it on Christmas morning. Worth it for the "Awesome!" the "Thanks, Mom!" the big brown eyes, and the bullshit.

CHAPTER SEVENTEEN
Storm Coming. Got Booze? Got Basement? Good to Go
Wednesday, 6:18 p.m.

Another natural disaster looms, but Wise Marj just texted me to say that she's all set.

"The hell with milk! I stocked up on beer."

My neighbor: I call her Wise Marj for a reason.

And I live in Ohio for a reason. When I figure it out, I'll let you know. We have no oceans, no landmarks, no real beaches, boring scenery, no oceans, hot, humid summers, long, gloomy winters, dull, rusty cities . . .

Did I mention we have no oceans?

However, we in the Buckeye State have one thing going for us: Aside from the occasional tornado, we usually don't get much in the way of natural disasters. Hurricanes, earthquakes, wildfires, tsunamis—our extremely boring, extremely landlocked state makes most of these particular acts of God difficult.

We are protected by our very mediocrity.

Until now. Enter the "derecho." The damn derecho.

Almost a year to the day after the last one, another one of these motherfuckers is on its way to our area. Or so they say.

What is a derecho, you ask? I wish I didn't know, but I do. A derecho is defined as a huge pain in the ass and, according to Wikipedia (so it must be true):

"A widespread, long-lived, straight-line wind storm that is associated with a land-based, fast-moving band of severe thunderstorms. Derechos can carry tornado-force winds and often deliver torrential rains and perhaps flash floods."

The last one cut a 700-mile swath of chaos across the Midwest and Mid-

Atlantic. They also called it a "land hurricane," and I'm pretty sure its eye centered over our property. It was an awful, epic adventure for my family, one that destroyed the roof, two ceilings, the yard, dozens of trees, the pool, two fences, and, most importantly, the basketball hoop and trampoline. Directly and indirectly, it rendered all three of our crappy cars useless.

Oh—and the husband lost a big chunk of his finger to a chainsaw mishap during cleanup. But it grew back.

Eventually.

We made many trips to Wise Marj's house, for water, for beer, and in 104-degree weather, we shuffled like crackheads, between her place, a packed hotel, a camper and a half-destroyed house with no functional plumbing.

There's a fine, fine line between "camping" and "homeless." That line has a name. Want to know what it is?

Flushing. That's right. I spent two complete weeks yelling:

"Do you have to poop? For the love of all that's holy, poop at the hotel! Poop while you can!"

Hahaha! Good times!

And now, about a year later, the meteorologists have been yelling derecho for two days, sweating and stammering and predicting The End.

This is not lost on the Hobo, who stares out the window with worried brown eyes, then roots around in the toy box for his flashlight. He was home during last year's storm when the trees fell on the house, the cars, the roof, the ceiling in his room—you get the point—and he now has a solid case of PTDDD: Post Traumatic Damn Derecho Disorder.

He finds the light and carries it to the cellar. In fact, we are *all* going down there, whether we want to or not. Because I said so.

Before heading downstairs, I pull up the Weather Channel app and the local news sites, and watch the meteorologists sweat, stammer and predict The End.

"Hey Princess!" I yell up the stairs to my daughter's room. "You're sleeping in the basement tonight!"

"Yeah. If it gets bad."

"No—no guessing in the middle of the night. You're sleeping in the basement."

"But, Mom!" she protests. "It's not even bad yet and I . . ."

"Get to the basement! *Now!*"

The Princess needs to learn: She has no choice. Anyway, we are Ohioans. Though we don't experience many disasters, we take them seriously. And if there's a weather threat, a Buckeye goes to the basement. It's pretty much a state law.

I learned this in the 1970s, back in the groovy day. When the weathermen forecasted a tornado and began sweating, stammering and predicting The End, my grandmother thumped a quick, heavy path between the blaring weather radio, the TV and the dining-room window. With worried blue eyes, she scanned the cornfields surrounding the house.

And if she saw even a hint of funnel clouds, flying cows, Jesus, Jesus on a flying cow . . .

"Get to the basement! *Now*!"

She grabbed the flashlight and we barreled down the stairs. And there, hunched amongst the boxes, canned tomatoes, and dusty Mason jars, we waited for The End.

After the rains stopped and the winds died down, Grandma dispatched my grandfather upstairs to assess the situation. He scanned the cornfields for funnels/flying cows/Jesus, and, seeing none of these, he'd call to us.

"All clear!"

"OK," said my grandmother, still clutching the flashlight. "We can go up."

We rose from the boxes, dusted off our rear ends and climbed the stairs.

I could never relax in a home without a cellar. And I'm worried about this impending storm, but I've been through it once.

Anyway, my grandparents taught me well: I've forced everyone down the stairs. And I've asked all the right questions:

"Do you have to poop? For the love of all that's holy. Poop now! Poop while you can!"

And even in the event of funnels/flying cows/Jesus, things will be alright. Roofs can be rebuilt. Trampolines can be replaced. Plumbing can be repaired, and trees and fingertips will grow back.

Eventually.

Plus, the Hobo has a flashlight, we have this basement, and best of all, Wise Marj bought beer, which she promises to share.

The hell with milk.

CHAPTER EIGHTEEN
Screwing. It Isn't Always Fun
Sunday, 9:50 a.m.

Three little words.

They are powerful, full of meaning and nuance. They'll stop you in your tracks, force you to contemplate your purpose in life, bring you to your knees with their significance. They have the strength to make or break any relationship.

Three little words.

"Some Assembly Required."

Sob

"Are you ready?" yells the husband, from upstairs.

Oh, for shit's sake. Can't he see I am very busy, here on the couch with my phone, thumbing through Pinterest for new Mason jar uses?

"What?!"

"We need to put Levi's bed together!" he hollers.

"He's fine!" I holler back.

"Dawn. He's been sleeping on the floor!"

"He has a mattress!" On the floor—like a crackhead.

Ah, crap. The husband is right. It happens. Occasionally.

Anyway, the boy's homeless/crackhead/hobo bed is probably my fault. Ever since the derecho/land hurricane/whatever-the-fuck-it-was hurled several large trees onto our house and poked holes through the roof and ceilings a year ago, I have been a little bit crazy, worried about more storms. Riddled with more crazy, I recently became convinced that trees would again fall on my son's room, poke through the roof and hurt him where he slept on his built-in, very high, *very near the ceiling* bunk.

This is not likely to happen: No trees remain. The storm took them all.

But I never let reality stop me, no sir.

So, in a PTSD frenzy, this crazy worried mama spent half a day industriously tearing down her son's bunk bed. Then, I figured, the trees—that no longer exist—would not poke through the ceiling and stab him. I pulled his mattress to the floor, where I figured he'd be safe. Hobo conditions, sure.

But safe, *stab-free* hobo conditions.

And I promptly forgot about it. Very busy, you see, with working, mothering, perpetually loading the dishwasher and looking at Pinterest, until the husband came home one day and noisily dragged in boxes. Large boxes. Large boxes with an alleged bed inside and three words:

"Some Assembly Required."

Sob

I've been studiously ignoring them. But it's Sunday and he's up there calling me now. I know he will pester me until we get this thing built, so I trudge up the steps to my homeless kid's room and "Some Assembly Required."

"Look! I've got everything ready to go for us!" says the husband. He's trying to lure me with faux happiness, I can tell. "Got everything we need. A screwdriver, the hammer, turned on a fan and the TV. . ."

"I don't see a 12-pack. We need a 12-pack."

"It's 10 a.m. Come on! Help me put this together. It won't take long."

Help me put this together, he says. It won't take long, he says.

Lies!

We don't fight much, he and I, except when faced with "Some Assembly Required." I am mechanically inclined, and, thanks to years of living single and dirt poor, pretty damn good with an Allen wrench and cheap furniture. Despite my mad particle-board skills, putting things together makes me sweaty, sore, and borderline homicidal. I was not blessed with the, how-you-say, "patience."

He, on the other hand, usually remains steady and even-tempered. He can handle basic home repair, a little auto-maintenance, yard work; plus he's an amazing father. Need a fence mended? Grass cut? Five giggling girls driven to cheerleading practice? He's your guy.

But he was not blessed with the, how-you-say, "following directions."

That's where I come in. So I pick up the sheet.

And, as Ikea is my witness, I am not making this up:

"1) To insert -21-(3) on S1 (3) and -22 (3), use -221 by placing it on -21 (-3) and -22 (-3), and knock it in with a hammer."

Hahaha!

Sob

We definitely need a 12-pack.

But it's 10 a.m., and we're out of beer because I finished it last night. So we begin, pulling out the wood and crushing the box.

We bend. We grunt. We pound. We screw. And not in any kind of fun way.

Forty-five minutes later, he stops to examine our progress. "Why does it look like that?" he asks. "Shouldn't that one board go across and not down?"

I am on the floor, bent into a pretzel, "inserting -21-(3) on S1 (3) and -22 (3), use -221 by placing it on -21 (-3) and -22 (-3), and knocking it in with a hammer," because I follow directions.

"You're over-thinking this!" I yell. "Don't think! Just follow the directions. Keep screwing!"

"But . . . "

"*Don't think! Just screw!*"

"OK! OK! Bossy McBitchypants!"

More bending. More grunting. More pounding. More screwing. Still not in any kind of fun way.

An hour of my life I'll never get back later, I stop working to read step 39-C of the instructions. He pokes me in the leg with a board. Hard.

"Ouch! Dammit! You hit me with the corner there. What are you doing?"

"Well, sorry, but I was thinking we could turn it around so . . . "

"*Don't think!*"

"Yessss, dear," he hisses.

I look back down at the instructions. But not before silently noticing the proliferation of sharp objects, conveniently located nearby.

We keep screwing, like a good couple should, and somehow, we manage. We refrain from stabbing each other and power through. Two hours, 759 screws, several thousand cuss words and exactly zero beers later, we're done. The boy's bed is finished, and I use my crazy PTSD superpowers to arrange it, ensuring he won't get stabbed by any non-existent wayward trees. We pull his homeless crackhead mattress off the floor, we place it onto the boards, and I ascertain that it is most assuredly *not near the ceiling*!

I make the bed and throw myself on top of the sheets.

"Gah! I am so sweaty and sore. Do not ask me to assemble anything for a long time. Like ever, *ever* again."

He stoops, picks up the screwdriver, stands up and smiles.

"That's fine, dear. But guess what?"

I eye his very long, very sharp tool. "What?"

Slowly, slowly, slowly, he raises the screwdriver.

Then, he turns and points it to the corner of the room.

Another box. The headboard.

Some Damn Assembly Required.

Sob
We will definitely need a 12-pack.

CHAPTER NINETEEN
Midwestern Saturday Night. Wake Me When It's Over
Saturday, 8:52 p.m.

It's a warm spring evening, and we of the "Too Old to Go to Bars" Club have opened up the shed, chased out a winter's worth of mice and pulled lawn chairs around a fire.

We're at the home of Wise Marj and Greg, our neighbors here in beautiful downtown Brownsville, Ohio (Motto: Indoor Plumbing Optional). During the fall and winter, we play cards at the kitchen table; in the spring and summer, we sit around a fire.

This is our Saturday night, and I will tell you: It is not much.

Then again, we are Ohioans—we really don't expect much.

The husband has parked himself in the chair beside me, and the kids are within texting distance, all of us soaked in the glow of cell phone screens, iPods, and the fire. A few beers rest at our feet, along with a big bag of potato chips.

Lucky, Marj and Greg's stinky and enthusiastic dog, wags around, whipping us with his tail, knocking over beers and resting his head in our laps. He's an all-around eager, adorable nuisance, and in case you can't tell, he's happy to see you.

He wonders: Perhaps you have a spare potato chip?

Across the fire in his chair, Greg does not share his dog's good humor. He's annoyed with the radio.

"This song sucks," he says. "Who is it?" An obscure blues tune plays, and its length and 18 bars of repetitiveness irritate him.

"It's that guy. You like him," replies Marj.

"What guy?"

I know who they're talking about: Stevie Ray Vaughn. But this is an enjoyable exchange, so I let them go on for a while, because it's free entertainment. And again—I don't expect much.

"That guy. You know . . . he's dead now," says Marj, cocking her head and scrunching her face in concentration. "Who is it? Who is that guy who died on our wedding day?"

"*I* did, Marj. I *died* a little inside on our wedding day," replies Greg.

She slaps him hard on the thigh. "Oh, shut up, you ass."

Matt walks out of the house and perches on the side of a lawn chair. He's 17, Marj and Greg's son, a lanky state track and cross-country champion. The first time I met him, at age 18 months, he hurled his baby bottle across the room and nailed me in the forehead.

It was love at first site.

I consider him a nephew, and these days, he specializes in verbal volleys.

"Ha ha! Look at you losers, sitting around a fire on a Saturday night!" he says.

I start to point out the irony that he is a senior in high school who has also stayed home on a Saturday night, but the husband beats me to the point.

"Shouldn't you be hanging around a fire with *your* friends, loser?"

I turn to Marj and Greg. "These kids don't seem to go out as much as we did."

"It's the cell phones and gadgets," Greg says. "They sit there, texting and Twittering each other at home, instead of getting together in real life."

I shake my head in disbelief. At Matt's age, I had one mission: Attend all parties.

It's good to have goals.

I also worked at McDonald's. But working interfered with my mission of attending all parties. So sometimes, I just didn't go to work.

Priorities. I had them.

The location of the get together really didn't matter. Where adults saw a field or an abandoned strip mine, we saw a party. Where they saw a tailgate, we saw a dance floor. We needed only wood and matches, because it was not a party without a bonfire. And a brawl. And possible police involvement.

Hey—parties that don't kill you only make you stronger. That was our idiotic mantra.

Twenty-five years ago, the drinking age was lower, times were different. We were young. We were lucky.

We were flat-out stupid.

Speaking of young and stupid, I glance over at Matt. He's athletic, true, but so skinny that a stiff wind could snap his bones. I think also of my 16-year-old daughter nearby—the one who's just started driving—and her little brother, both in the living room.

Yes. Twittering in the front of the TV is a fine place for them to spend Saturday night.

I pull my mind out of the cloud of worry, back to the present, to the bonfire burning now.

Matt hangs around for a while, and the five of us talk, laugh and exchange insults. "Green River" comes on the radio, leading off a whole set of CCR, and Greg is visibly relieved. He loves CCR.

The sky fades from blue to black, and we slowly stop feeding the fire, letting the yellow flames die to orange embers. We sip our beers, eat our chips, talk ourselves silent.

I glance back down at my phone.

"Holy crap. It's after 11. We better get home."

Weekend or not, my possibly perimenopausal monkey-mind will wake itself at 4:30 a.m. I'm already facing less than five hours of sleep by the time we get settled.

We fold the chairs, kill the fire and pick up the trash and bottles. Lucky the dog, ever hopeful, ever smelly, sniffs around the remnants.

He wonders: Perhaps you left a potato chip?

Another Saturday night has ended. We only enjoyed a few beers between us, a couple of hours to relax.

But even in its mediocrity, this was the very highlight of my week. After all, I am an Ohioan. I really don't expect much.

CHAPTER TWENTY
Brownsville, Ohio. Motto: Bring Your Own Generator
Sunday, 12:22 p.m.

Welcome to Beautiful Downtown Brownsville. Population . . . oh . . . approximately . . . maybe . . . 30.

Thirty cows, that is.

30 cows, zero milk.

Got milk? Good. I'd like to borrow some, because we have none. We ran out the other day, and Brownsville has no store. Neither do we have a post office, a gas station or a pizza shop. No one will even *deliver* pizza here. Moving to the country? Please. I implore you. Know this: Pizza shops don't deliver outside a certain radius, and you, Brownsville—you're outside that radius. Way outside.

A trip to pick up a loaf of bread or a gallon of milk requires $20 worth of gas and a four-hour commitment. Thirsty? Forget buying beer, unless you're up for 60 minutes, round-trip. Our town founders were teetotaling senior citizens, apparently, so there's quite a few options for church, but if you want a bottle of wine, you better book a flight.

Twenty years now. I've been here 20 years. Still can't get used to living on the frontier. I thought about it again the other day, on a quest for groceries, staring out the windshield at the lovely scenery: a barn, some cows, a field. And look! Over there! A field, a barn, some cows. Repeat. Ad infinitum.

Statistics rank Ohio as the ninth most populated state. Evidently, they're counting the cows.

I grew up in New Springfield, Ohio—a town of equal size. Same kind of dirt roads, same 3:1 cow/human ratio, but things were different. My hometown had a store. There was a post office. There was a gas station.

There was a pizza shop with—joy of joys!—a Pac-Man machine.

Here, we have none of those. In Brownsville, we're lucky to have electricity, and often, we don't. This is the town that time and American Electric Power forgot. Minor storms, slight breezes, cow flatulence—all bring sufficient wind disturbance to disrupt the weak, archaic power lines stretched across trees. The many, many, many trees.

However, like good pioneers, we know the art of survival. We're well-versed in flashlights and candles, and—armed with only bucket and rain water—we can flush a mean toilet. During storm season, the hills buzz with generators and chainsaws, a constant hum echoing across the mobile homes, abandoned houses, chained-out dogs. We are hearty stock, women working alongside the men to release fallen limbs from our roofs, cars, trailers. We have no choice in this; there simply aren't enough county workers to cover the area after a storm. Anyway, their services are much needed 15 miles north, in town, by the Target and the Walmart, where money is made, where Brownsvillians buy milk.

I can't imagine why, but no one wants to visit us. We even put in a pool—that didn't work. I'm thinking of building a casino. It probably wouldn't matter. The phone calls would remain the same:

Me: "Hey! We're having a cookout this weekend. You don't need to bring anything. Just come on over!"

Friend: *Awkward silence*

Me: "Free beer!"

Friend: *More silence*

Me: "Hello? Did you hear me? I said we're having a cookout!"

Friend: "Yeah. Uh . . . your place is too far away. Why don't you come over here?"

Me: *SLAM*

I don't have cookouts anymore.

I also don't have friends anymore.

And I was just about done with it, pioneer life. Tired of lacking milk and post office; sick to death of driving for pizza; absolutely finished with reporting power outages for the electric company to ignore. I had serious thoughts of packing it all up and moving back to the 'burbs, with its heady promise of utilities and pizza and functioning plumbing.

Then I heard it: News so exciting that I almost dropped my chainsaw. Hang onto your flush bucket, folks: Word is they're building a dollar store, half a mile down the road.

People. That is pretty much as good as it gets.

Oh, dollar stores, how I love you, popping up in small towns everywhere, supplying country folk with canned goods, double-A batteries, plastic lawn furniture.

I can't quite believe it. It's almost too good to be true. Imagine the convenience of a store in the same county! The joy of buying milk, bread, perhaps (dare I dream?) eggs, and returning home the very same day!

Think about the proximity to toilet paper, to laundry detergent, to cheap sunglasses!

I think I just peed a little.

What's next? Will we, the Brownsvillians, someday be able to purchase local gasoline? Order a pizza? Holy Heineken—will we one day have the ability to pick up a six pack without an airline ticket?

A girl can only dream.

I'm waiting for you and your black-and-yellow goodness, dollar store. But until then, chainsaw in hand, generator at the ready, I guess I'll just power through like the stoic redneck I've become. And I'll keep on trekking, past the cows, and into town. For everything.

Yep. Saddle up the horses, Pa, we need Charmin.

Allow four to six weeks for delivery.

CHAPTER TWENTY-ONE
Just Bought Filet Mignon at the Dollar Store. Will Report My Findings
Sunday, 5:21 p.m.

Filet mignon. Dollar store.

These are frightening words, when side by side. But in my lifetime I've experienced many frightening things—childbirth, Miley Cyrus, the entire presidency of George W. Bush. And though terrifying, the proof of this "meat product" is also irrefutable: I'm standing here in the harsh yellow light near the frozen goods of our new dollar store, staring in open-mouthed wonder at a $5.95 two-pack of bacon-wrapped "Filet Mignon."

"Filet Mignon" indeed. I grab the package and scan the ingredients: water, salt, bacon, beef. I worry a little about their definition of "beef," but then again, I am desperate and on a frantic mission for food. I have three hamburgers and four mouths to feed tonight, and even with the unfortunate math skills afforded to a word person, I can see that won't be enough. Also, we are having a very special guest for dinner:

Our daughter.

Oh, sure. She still lives with us, but now that she's driving, an actual sighting of Her Highness is as rare as spotting, say, the Easter Bunny, or an endangered bird.

The Princess's presence isn't the only thing that has sent me rushing to the store. I want to make it a special evening because it's also Device-Free Family Fun Night, which, in an optimistic and completely delusional mood, I invented a few months ago. Usually held on Sundays, DFFFN is a delightful event wherein all family members are prohibited from using electronic devices, and we spend quality time together acting crabby because we can't use electronic devices.

"Don't forget—Sunday is Device-Free Family Fun Night!" I tell the kids each weekend.

"Oh, Mom! Not again!" is their enthusiastic response.

Ah, how they love it.

I think about all this, still standing by the freezer and holding the questionable meat in my hand. It will be an undeniably special night, what with the absence of electronics and the presence of the Princess. It can only improve with the addition of "Filet Mignon" from the "dollar store." I throw the package into the shopping basket. Then, for shits and giggles, I thumb over to my phone's Facebook app and post the news.

"Just bought a filet mignon from the dollar store, out of both morbid curiosity and desperation. Will report my findings."

Fwoom! My notifications icon fires up as red as a slaughterhouse.

"Better make gravy!" comments Rick.

"You must be in the pet food section!" writes Melissa.

"Make sure your bathrooms are well-stocked!" advises Jonathon.

And on and on goes the intelligent social commentary from Facebook friends, many of whom assert that I'll be eating horse meat, and react as if I've personally gone out to pasture and sliced off a chunk of prize thoroughbred.

"Neigh on the horse meat!" says Raymond.

I drive home and carry the alleged equine into the house, where the Princess and the Hobo sit sulking in their rooms in anticipation of Device-Free Family Fun Night. I remove the plastic, put the meat in a pan and fire up the broiler.

Beep-beep-beep-beep-beep!

Smoke detectors, I've decided, should really come with two settings: a normal setting, and an "It's OK! I'm just cooking dinner!" setting. That's the way it goes at our place, especially when I make bacon, or anything with bacon such as a bacon-wrapped filet mignon. As I've said before, I am bacon-challenged. I've tried frying it in a skillet.

Beep-beep-beep-beep-beep!

I've tried baking bacon in the oven.

Beep-beep-beep-beep-beep!

I've even tried to cook bacon on the grill.

Beep-beep-beep-beep-beep!

Is it a house fire? Or is it a meal? It is both—with bacon.

On this particular Device-Free Family Fun Night, I run from oven to stove-top to smoke detector, finishing dinner and frantically waving a dish towel, which is my standard method of smoke disbursement. I could pull the battery from the alarm while cooking, but if I do so, I might never replace it. Removing and replacing the battery require a chair or a stool and some effort, and as a rule, I am against effort. I avoid effort whenever possible.

Beep-beep-beep-beep-beep!

As the filet finishes smoking in the broiler, the noise and hubbub draw the children from their respective rooms. But the husband doesn't even glance up from the TV.

"It's OK, guys," he says. "Mom's just cooking dinner."

"What did she make?" asks the Princess, pulling up her chair.

"Filet mignon," I say, "from the dollar store."

The boy covers his mouth. "Ewww-uhh!"

"Don't you guys want to try it?" I ask, knowing the answer. Filet mignon does not fall into their four main food groups of pizza, pizza rolls, pizza Hot Pockets and hamburgers.

"Ewww-uhh!" they yell in unison.

In the interest of keeping the peace—and journalistic integrity—I decide to eat it myself. I have no idea what it will taste like. Beef? Chicken? Secretariat? But I'm an adventurous sort. So I slice a piece, lift the fork, open my mouth, place it on my tongue, slowly chew, and there and then I decide that the mystery meat is . . .

. . . fine.

Although my Facebook friends are vigorously rooting otherwise, I report back to them that the filet tastes decent, and that I survived, I thrived, I lived to tell.

Do I feel nauseous? Do I get sick? Do I explode from either end? Nay. Or neigh, as the case may be.

I knew I'd be OK. The dollar store and the "beef" company had surely sold me a primo product, and had my best interests at heart. Bunch of old white guys? Probably billionaires? Absolutely!

The meat industry has always been known for its ethics and honesty.

And all things considered, I think the dollar store DNA tastes just fine. Yummy, even.

If it's horse meat, it is good horse meat.

CHAPTER TWENTY-TWO
Meet Our Dog. She's Kind of an Asshole
Monday, 8:32 a.m.

You've met black Labs, yellow Labs and chocolate Labs.

Now, meet the Meth Lab.

Go ahead. Tell her to get down. She'll scratch your flesh to bloody ribbons.

Tell her to stop barking. She'll bark until there's hearing loss—in the next county.

Tell her to get a stick. She will bring you a mid-sized maple tree.

Then, she'll spin around with said tree in her mouth, taking out your knees Tonya Harding-style, whereupon you will slam onto the driveway, screaming in agony, causing your spouse to rush over in an alarmed fashion to ask what's wrong. The Meth Lab long gone, you'll direct an epic string of expletives at your mate and the fucking horse he rode in on, all the while blinded and vomiting from pain.

That's what you get for owning the Meth Lab, a whirling dervish, a veritable ball of spastic energy loosely described as "dog."

It's not entirely your fault; you were fooled. As a puppy, the Meth Lab looked remarkably like a sweet little black Lab. You couldn't believe your luck, finding such a fine example of the Labrador breed, fenced, with several dozen other dogs, in the muddy yard of a run-down, single-wide trailer.

Oh, sure, her human "owners" smacked of state of assistance; sure, her mother was a raging, angry-looking mutt; absolutely, her several dozen siblings resembled malnourished pit-bulls. But hey, you're a live-and-let-live, tree-hugging liberal type of gal. Who were you to judge?

Also, she was free.

The target of your affections was the pure-bred-appearing, soft-black-furred puppy with huge brown eyes, quivering in a docile, affectionate, free-to-a-good home fashion at your feet.

So you took the adorable, calm pup to your house. That was your first mistake. And you wormed her. That was your second mistake.

Then, you fed her. That was your final mistake.

Because little did you know that "dogs" like these only behave well for two reasons: 1) To trick dummies into adopting them; and 2) They are sickly, and riddled with worms.

Parasites gone, belly full of food, your mellow, calm, black Lab-looking puppy soon started feeling better. And she grew. And she changed.

Her body expanded at an alarming rate—her ears shrunk, her legs lengthened—until she resembled the melee of breeds exhibited by her mother, her siblings and the county's 7,000 other "dogs" of the Heinz 57 variety.

She began chewing—everything. She began barking—at everyone. She began mauling—everything and everyone. And then she went crazy:

You watched in abject terror as she launched her formidable mass at all your visitors' cars. Nice cars. New cars.

Now? Scratched cars.

You blanched in horror as she jumped up unexpectedly at the kennel, sinking her razor-sharp claws into the papery thighs of an old lady. The woman, who took blood-thinning medication, began bleeding profusely.

Somewhere, she still bleeds.

You cowered in shame—then wanted to rip your eyeballs out—after witnessing her hump a stuffed animal. Repeatedly. You Googled "holy shit my female puppy humps" and discovered that girl dogs hump sometimes, too. You wish you didn't know this. But you do.

One thing quickly became clear: Owning a Meth Lab requires patience, a different mindset and a much stronger shock collar than you need with a yellow, black or chocolate Lab. Other things that help include weapons, tranquilizers and sedation—for you.

That's right. As we saw from the genius decision you made when you adopted this crackhead "dog," you and your canine are special, as in a "Special Needs," or "need-to-wear-a-helmet" kind of way. See below, Special Friend, for your Handy Meth Lab FAQ:

What do I feed the Meth Lab?

Don't bother, for they eat *anything*. Furniture, poop, rocks, toddlers; some think of these as inedible. Meth Labs consider them the four main food groups.

Can I give my Meth Lab treats?

Yes, but there's no need to be choosy; the Meth Lab will happily snack from a full cat litter box with no digestive issues. But an expensive butcher bone will cause her to explode from both ends.

How long does a Meth Lab usually live?

In general, far too long.

How do I train the Meth Lab?

Again, don't bother. As we've seen from our previous attempts at training, commands like "Down!" "Quiet!" and "Don't blow out my knees with a tree!" mean nothing to the Meth Lab. They are just suggestions, mere background noise in a crackhead "dog's" day of destruction.

Should I enroll a Meth Lab in obedience classes?

Yes, if you enjoy such activities as throwing money into an active fire pit.

How do I pet a Meth Lab?

Very carefully. Preferably, from a distance, maybe with a stick, or perhaps have someone else do it, such as a mortal enemy. Remember: These "dogs" throw their heart, soul, teeth, claws and entire body mass into everything they do, including affection. This means anyone attempting to pet them will likely lose skin, hair, toenails, a limb—you get my point. Someone will bleed, and it won't be the Meth Lab.

Are there any special medical concerns for the Meth Lab?

No, but there are for you. See info re: teeth, blood loss, Tonya Harding/tree/knees above.

If you follow all these tips, your pup will thrive and grow rapidly, achieving full-fledged, psycho Meth Lab status. You can't leave her alone or take her anywhere; your friends and family have stopped visiting your home. But that's OK, as you now have more time for your developing drinking problem. As a Meth Lab owner, you'll simultaneously acquire both high blood pressure and a dull resignation to your fate, because you've heard that only the first 18 years of the Meth Lab's life are the hardest. You may learn to love—or at least tolerate—this crazy crackhead breed of "dog," that pounces you, scratches you, destroys cars, bankrupts you, Tonya-Hardings your knees, and licks you with litter-box breath. After all, she still has the huge brown eyes and soft black fur.

And you'll never, ever give her up, for one simple, pure, solitary reason: No one else will take her.

CHAPTER TWENTY-THREE
Golf. Hideous Shorts Required
Monday, 2:23 p.m.

Golf—what's not to love? You're outside, you're drinking beer, and you're around lots of happy, relaxed men, many of whom may buy more beer.

Everybody wins.

Each spring it happens: I get the Big Idea. I really should just lie down until these ideas go away, but I never do.

No, I get it in my head that this will be The Year, the one wherein I Learn to Play Golf.

Now, I am a middle-aged white woman with a big, wide rear-end and plenty of hideous yet sensible shorts. So you'd think I'd already know how to golf.

But I don't. For many years now, I've engaged in the process of just learning how to hit the ball, or "drive" I guess the kids call it these days. This is much harder than it looks—for me, anyway.

So every March, I drag out my clubs, a gift the husband bought me one year after I excitedly told him my Big Idea:

"I want to learn to play golf!"

He's heard many of my "I want to learn!" Big Ideas: drawing, painting, piano-playing, jewelry-making. Most of these I've taught to myself, or forgotten about; all of these have left us lighter in the wallet and heavy on accumulated Big Idea supplies.

So, being the smart, sweet, frugal man he is, when I said, "Golf!" he went out and bought me a set of clubs at a garage sale.

And that's fine with me, because the red-and-white, 30-year-old Wilson golf bag looks cool and kind of retro, and also meets what in my eyes ranks as the Most Important Golf Requirement:

It matches my shoes.

Ah . . . shoes.

Anyway, he bought me the cool matching bag and a bunch of clubs, all of which had numbers—3, 5, 9—that signified nothing to me, although I did recognize the putter from playing Putt-Putt. I can kick some Putt-Putt ass.

He put a tee and ball down in the grass, and began showing me how to drive. He taught me how to grip the club, and he demonstrated the swing, the "all in the hips," then he set me up and came up behind me to lead my body through a swing, whereupon he faux-humped me and I punched him in the nuts. Lesson over.

His obsessive faux-humping is a chapter unto itself.

But I didn't let the humping stop me, no. I am nothing if not dedicated to activities that involve drinking beer outside.

And so it goes that each spring, I grab my garage-sale golf bag, dust it off and head for the driving range, a.k.a. the front yard, where I tiptoe my way around a winter's worth of accumulated dog turds. Picturing outdoor fun, beer and happy men, I set up my tee, trying to get my mind and body ready for another sweaty and futile session of trying to hit the ball.

I swing. I miss.

I swing again. I miss, and also plow up dirt.

I swing a third time. I miss, I plow up dirt and then cuss a sailor-string of expletives.

Stopping myself from flinging the club into the woods, I draw a deep breath and re-examine my stance and form. I take a slow swing back, pivot my hips and bring the driver down, down, down towards the tee, the way the husband showed me, right before the faux-hump.

And that's when it hits me: It's the boobs. My boobs are in the way.

Not that they are particularly big or impressive. But somehow the angle of my arms gets all wrapped up, smashed and stopped by my breasts. I should have remembered this dilemma, because I had the same problem last year, and the year before that, and the year before that.

I sit down on the front porch step to think for a minute. I know that other women are successful with the game of golf; I've heard of the LPGA, and I've seen tons of other local ladies with big wide rear-ends, golf clubs and hideous, sensible shorts. No matter their size, they do not have seem to have this tit-entanglement problem.

If I asked him, the husband would happily help me again, but it would end, of course, in a faux-hump for me and a nut-punch for him. And I don't know much about sports, but I do know this: Golf is not about pain. Or humping.

Golf is about drinking beer outside.

This thought inspires me. I stand and walk back over to the tee, set up the ball, take a whack.

I swing, I miss—boobs. I swing again. I miss, and also plow up dirt—more boobs. I swing a third time. I miss.

You guessed it: boobs. I'm done.

For now, anyway. Before I Happy-Gilmore my entire set of garage-sale clubs into the weeds, I better quit.

That's OK. As I pack up my bag, the sun warms my face, reminding me that the weather will turn nice in a month or two. I'll once more be able to drink beer outside doing something I'm actually good at: sitting around the pool.

Thus ends my season of golf.

Tiptoeing back through the dog turds, I realize that I will probably get this Big Idea again next year, and although I enjoy learning things on my own, I should probably take some real golf lessons from a pro to figure out this boob dilemma. If not, I might as well get rid of my golf bag.

But, hey—it matches my shoes.

Ah . . . shoes.

CHAPTER TWENTY-FOUR
Empty Wallet, Drained Gas Tank, Blown Speakers. Yep, I Have a Sixteen-Year-Old
Wednesday, 6:56 a.m.

I know I have a daughter. Somewhere.

I haven't seen her for a while, but I know she exists because my blush is missing. Again.

It's not, of course, the $4 Maybelline blush I bought during the Clinton administration—that's readily available at the top of my makeup bag. No, this is the $33 Nars blush I ogled, debated over and felt horribly guilty about; the very item whose purchase still lurks on my Visa bill.

Yes, I have a daughter. A teenage daughter, to be exact. It's early in the morning, but the missing makeup was actually my second reminder of her presence, after my ice-cold shower that resulted from an empty hot water tank.

I stomp out of the bathroom, looking for the girl so I can ask her, in a patient, motherly way, exactly where the hell my good blush is. She's easy to track. I just follow the trail of shoes, backpacks and microwave popcorn bags.

"Princess!" I yell up the stairs.

Nothing.

"Oh, *Princess*!!"

Still nothing. She's not here right now, of course. She's seldom here. She's 16—and a half. I really haven't seen her for six months.

When she is home, she's in her room almost constantly, very busy with her social life, her iPhone, her three-hour grooming process. Just yesterday, she was a raggedy little monkey who had to be bribed into the tub with handfuls of candy, but now, she drains Lake Erie with her showers. If you hear the blow dryer, you know she's home, and you'll find her upstairs, waving a Conair around her head in an urgent, determined fashion.

I don't hear a blow dryer today, and I don't feel like yelling to an empty room anymore. So I give up and decide to send her a text—our main method of communication these days.

"Exactly where the hell is my *good blush*?" I write, in a patient, motherly way.

"Oh sorry!" she texts back. "I borrowed it. It's in my room. Sorry!"

Imagine that. I figured it was up there, right beside, no doubt, my powder, my hairspray and my eyeliner.

I finish getting ready, applying what little makeup she's left to me. I grab my phone, coat, purse and keys, head out to the car, and start it up.

Fuel: E

I definitely have a teenage daughter.

"Highs today in the mid-30s, with lows in the FERRBLE-FERRBLE-FERBBB!!"

Who's drained my gas tank and blown my stereo speakers.

I can see it's time to text her again—in a patient, motherly way.

"Please don't turn the Honda's speakers up so loud and why didn't you tell me it was *out of gas*?!"

"Oh sorry!" she writes back. "Guess I forgot. Sorry!"

Shaking my head, I put the car in drive, head down the driveway and onto the highway, where I begin scanning the sides of the road. Even when I know she's not at the wheel, I still sub-consciously look for her everywhere—on the street, in the ditch, at every accident I pass. I'm amazed she's driving. I'm proud she's driving.

I am horrified she's driving.

This is a kid who really can't operate a dishwasher. She's not even that great at riding a bike, let alone negotiating 3,000 pounds of steel down a highway at 55 miles per hour.

Driving—or riding shotgun with friends—she's out there every chance she gets. She goes to school, to cheerleading, with the girls, and especially, with her boyfriend. The last place she wants to go?

Home.

And though she would disagree, mostly I let her run. I understand these things: friends, boys and freedom. I remember when the road meant independence. At this stage of my life, driving only means responsibility—just another exhilarating trip to work or Walmart.

Speaking of such excitement, I spot the gas station up ahead. I pull in, stop the car, cut the ignition and glance into the rearview mirror to check my makeup in the gathering daylight. I ascertain that I look fine, if decidedly blush-free. Pale skin, blonde hair, brown eyes—to see my reflection is to see her reflection. She's a younger, smoother, firmer, altogether better version of me.

As I climb out and begin pumping gas, my mind flashes back to the little girl, to the tiny monkey—not so long ago—who never left my side.

"C'mon Mom," she said. "Let's play cards!"

I was many months pregnant with her brother, crabby, exhausted and above all, card-gamed out.

"We just played four hands in a row," I said. "Mom's tired."

She crossed her arms, threw herself back onto the couch cushions and furrowed her forehead. "You better spend time with me now!"

I played cards again—of course I did—all the while smiling to myself, because it was just the type of thing I would have said. We are exactly alike.

Which, somehow, makes us completely different.

I know that's why we butt heads, we argue. We argue about money and clothes and boyfriends and curfews; we argue about homework and colleges and stereo volume and the size of her jeans. We argue about cell phones and her messy room. We argue because she is never home anymore.

I finish pumping, walk inside the store to pay, open my wallet and find that it's time to send another patient, motherly text.

"Can you please tell me when you take the *last of my flippin' cash*?!"

"Oh—sorry! Dad said to take it out of your purse. Sorry!"

Sorry. She's sorry, all right.

She empties my gas tank, steals my makeup, uses up the hot water and blows my speakers. She spends all my money, and then she asks for more.

She baby-sits her brother, gets straight As, has great manners and treats people with kindness. She does her chores—sometimes even without threats. A cheerleader since third grade, she can back-flip across an entire football field. She flies.

She is difficult and wonderful and exasperating and amazing and many times—damn near impossible.

She is 16. And a half. I miss her already.

CHAPTER TWENTY-FIVE
Road Trips. The First 29 Hours Are the Hardest
Saturday, 10:20 a.m.

We've been on the road for four hours now.

I've had to pee—for four hours now.

"Of course you do," he says.

You're damn right, of course I do. I am a 44-year-old woman who drinks 64 ounces of water and four cups of coffee a day. I possess a bladder that has been cheerily pummeled by two fetuses. If I am conscious, I have to pee. If I am upright, I have to pee.

If I am breathing, I have to pee.

But he ain't stopping. I know this because:

"I *ain't stopping*!"

He tells me, repeatedly. The husband, Swervy McDangerPants, and I have been married for 18 years, together for 20. He has a plan, a mission, and he's mashed down the pedal. I know this man. He means it.

He ain't stopping.

We're heading to our family vacation at approximately Mach 2, just the Hobo, the Princess, the husband and I. Grab a ceiling handle and join us—won't you?—as we swerve dangerously through Virginia.

I'm in the passenger seat, legs crossed, postponing the inevitable. To forget the rising, sloshing tide in my own personal Virginia, I've been writing here on my phone, but the curves and screen-staring are making me carsick. So I've just closed my eyes and slipped into a lovely dream in which I've rushed into a clean white restroom, unzipped my pants, sat down and . . .

"*Hey!*" yells the Princess, headphones in her ears. She's simultaneously listening to music and playing an iPhone trivia game. "Who did that

80

painting—the 'Mona Lisa'? Wait. I know. Leonardo DiCaprio."

"Um, I think it's DaVinci," I tell her. "Leonardo DaVinci is who you want."

Squeeze. Contract. Squeeze.

It's a good thing she woke me up. I came very close to christening the car seat.

I turn to Swervy. "I really have to pee. Can we stop? Like, sometime this millennium?"

He grips the wheel, his knuckles grow whiter. "Well, sorry, but I *ain't stopping!*"

Seriously. Why do I bother asking?

And it's getting even harder to maintain bladder control, what with Swervy's constant gazing at the Mapquest sheets in his lap. He specializes in multi-tasking while driving. Or so he thinks. I decide that he could use some of my input.

"I sure wish I had a little driver's ed. wheel and brake pedal on my side," I tell him, "so I could help you do all the things you do while you're supposed to be driving."

"I wish I had a fly swatter," he replies, "or some duct tape."

I look over at him, narrowing my eyes. He doesn't appreciate my helpful instruction. "I just like to help you with your driving."

He gives me a sideways grin. "You just like being a pain in my ass."

He is correct. But maybe I should give him some more direction.

"Well, perhaps it's not the best time to peruse the Mapquest papers," I tell him, "being that you're two inches from the car in front of you and going 80 miles an hour."

"I liked you better when you were asleep," he says. "Anyway, I'm a policeman, alright? I do this kind of stuff for a living."

Speed? Tailgate? Read while driving? These are the things I want to say, but I don't. I bite my tongue.

Squeeze. Contract. Squeeze.

I stare out the window at the gray-green blur, and watch the cars beside us; hundreds of Ohio families, it seems, all going to the beach. I bet a good 75 percent of these women have water in their greater Virginias.

And 100 percent of the men wish for duct tape. But they ain't stoppin'.

Whee! Squeeze. Contract. Squeeze. What a ride we're having here, on account of these hills and Swervy's veering all over the road.

"Why don't you pick a lane—any lane?"

"Hey. There's 18 feet of roadway, I use all 18 feet," he replies. "Anyway, who's driving this boat? Me, or you?"

Driving this boat? More like "piloting this jet." Again, that's what I want to say, but again, I bite my tongue.

My tongue. It bleeds.

"Oh!" hollers the Hobo from the backseat. "I'm going to throw up!"

The husband grips the wheel tighter. "Of course you are."

This is unwelcome—but not unexpected—news from the boy, who was quietly playing games on his iPod. Silence from him is not necessarily a good sign. Anyway, I should have checked on him sooner: Road-ralphing is his car-ride tradition.

I crane my neck back to look at him. It's early in the day, but already that kid is covered in Dorito dust. The $3.89 bag of Cool Ranch? The one that was supposed to last all the way down south? Nothing but bright orange MSG-crumbs covering his face, his shirt, his hands, his sister.

He's not supposed to eat them all like that. He's also supposed to stop playing iPod in the car when his stomach starts to hurt, when his motion sickness kicks in.

But he ate the chips. He played on his iPod. He's going to throw up.

And we have another problem.

"Ahhh! We're out of bags!"

I frantically rummage around the glove compartment for the stash of Walmart sack/barf bags that we keep on hand for the Hobo's routine. I glance back at him, his face growing ever-greener, his Cool Ranch-covered hands clutching his stomach. In a panic, I turn to the husband.

But he keeps his eyes on the road, a white-knuckled grip on the wheel.

"Well I *ain't stoppin'!*" he says.

Plan B. I shout to my teenage daughter, the Princess, hoping for some help. Ha ha! I said "teenage daughter'" and "help" in the same sentence. I am so funny sometimes.

"Hey!" I yell. "Do you have a McDonald's bag back there or something? Levi is going to throw up!"

No response. Honestly, I am not sure why I bother, but I try again.

"Laura!" I yell. "Do you have a bag back there? The Hobo is getting sick!"

Still nothing. She is directly behind me in the car, so it's difficult to turn completely around and choke her, er, catch her eye. But I can see my son back there, diagonally from me and doubled over in Dorito-dusted misery.

He's going to blow.

"*Hey Princess! Do you have a McDonald's bag or something? Your brother is going to puke!!!*" I scream.

"Huh?" she asks. "Did you say something? I can't hear you. I have my headphones in!"

Risking death, tempting fate, I undo my seat belt and hoist my body up and around, searching the back seat for something, *anything* that could serve as a possible yack sack. There are sandwich bags. There are book bags. There are damn-sure Doritos bags. But there is not one suitable barf bag.

I glance over at the boy. His head's in his lap now—he's reaching critical mass. I plop back down in my seat and turn to Swervy.

"You *have* to stop, on the side of the road or something. We have nothing for him."

"Rest stop—one mile. I cannot *believe* we have to stop. Make it quick, son!"

Finally, blessedly, he pulls into the rest area. The Hobo and I both get unbuckled before the vehicle stops, and I round the car, grab his hand and we sprint to the restroom, where he quickly loses his Doritos into a State of Virginia-purchased toilet.

There's $3.89 worth of MSG I'll never see again.

He finishes, and we head to the sink, where he rinses his mouth and I wash him down. We walk out of the ladies room.

"Hey Mom—look! Vending machines! Can I get something?"

I glance over at him, and he quickly looks down at the ground. Apparently, my eyes answered his question.

We get back in the car and buckle up. The husband puts it in drive and swerves dangerously out of the parking lot.

"I hope you got it all out of there, son, because I *ain't stoppin'* again!"

The Hobo wordlessly turns on his iPod, while the head-phoned Princess, oblivious to the whole incident, bobs her head and sings. Swervy mashes the pedal, merging out of the rest stop. Only several hundred miles to go! We hit I-77 southbound at Mach 2.

And as soon as I see the sign:

"Next Rest Area: 79 miles"

I realize it.

I have to pee. Of course I do.

CHAPTER TWENTY-SIX
The Five Stages of Vacation Grief
Monday, 10:32 a.m.

It's Monday and I'm happy.

As you know, "Monday" and "happy" don't usually go together. So my great mood means I'm either A) drunk, or B) on vacation, and I'm not drunk, so I must be on vacation—the only week of the year that Friday sucks, and Monday rocks.

Despite this backwards progression of despair, every year, I do it anyway. I take a week off, eager to get to the beach, overjoyed to be out of my cubicle, thrilled on Monday, and devastated on Friday. I have a name for this phenomenon. Please—read on for your handy guide to the Five Stages of Vacation Grief:

Denial:

Toes in the water, ass in the sand. It's your first day at the beach, and you stare out into the ocean, troubles slipping away with each receding wave. You have a dim awareness of a previous life in some sad fly-over state, but you choose to swallow these thoughts down, down, down with your first sip of Corona, along with the vague idea of going home and back to work next week.

What are these things called "home" and "work"? You laugh at such silly words!

Bargaining:

Feeling spiritual from the water, the sand and the beauty, you have conversations with God. "God," you say, "Please let me stay here. I don't need a house . . . or a job . . . or a family—I'll work on a shrimp boat and sleep alone on the beach. Like a bum. It will be fine."

God doesn't answer.

You have another beer.

Anger:

Why? Dammit, why do I voluntarily live in a place where my nostrils freeze shut six months a year when I could live on the coast? This you ask yourself while fuming and stomping down the shore, questioning your life choices and hating the locals, what with their smiles and tans and wide-open nostrils. *Other people get to live by the beach. Other people get to go to the beach every day.*

Be calm, my friend, for you should have learned long ago: other people suck.

Depression:

Reality sets in. You don't live at the beach. No—you're an imposter, a tourist, and only here temporarily. Worse, you have to leave soon, even though you don't want to go. It's in this miserable frame of mind that you come to one conclusion: Life is too short to live in Ohio/Nebraska/fill in your own pathetic landlocked state here.

Acceptance:

Alas. There's nothing you can do. That's it, it's over, and you must get back to maintain the mortgage and health care policy. So pack up your clothes, your smile, your will to live, and slouch on-board the plane, because before you know it, the wheels will touch down and you'll arrive home to the drudgery, endless to-do lists, and soul-killing routine that make up the average adult life.

Hey. At least the next time you feel happy at the beginning of the week and sad at the end, you'll know you're not drunk—but perhaps you should be—because you're experiencing the Five Stages of Vacation Grief: Denial, Bargaining, Anger, Depression and Acceptance. Otherwise known as Monday, Tuesday, Wednesday, Thursday, and Friday.

Stay strong, weary traveler, for it will be difficult to ease back into the misery of everyday existence. I recommend wine, more denial, and sobbing quietly in your cubicle.

Until next year.

CHAPTER TWENTY-SEVEN
Rustic Camping. It Seemed Like a Good Idea at the Time
Tuesday, 8:45 a.m.

They call it "rustic camping."

I call it stupid camping.

There's a fine, fine line between "rustic camping" and "homeless." That line is called "indoor plumbing."

Nonetheless, thousands of otherwise intelligent people pay campground owners perfectly good U.S. dollars every single weekend, all for the privileges of *not* sleeping in a bed, *not* having adequate shelter, and *not* using a working toilet.

And, over cans of Coors Light one night, a group of old friends and I decided it would be a hoot to take all our kids rustic camping. To get back to nature and whatnot.

This would not turn out to be one of our better schemes. But, like many concepts hatched by way of cheap American beer, it seemed like a great idea at the time.

So it was that one hot, balmy afternoon a few weeks later, this same group of friends—the Tony Carosella party, the Jimmy Powell party and us, the Joel Weber party—packed for the stupid, um, "rustic camping" trip by loading up the necessities: tents, food, bottled water and Coors Light.

A fourth family, the Bob Walsh party (a.k.a. the punks) decided to come with us, but opted against rustic camping and made reservations at the campground's fancy, air-conditioned, decidedly non-rustic lodge, complete with two pools and several actual working toilets.

The four groups met up at Salt Fork State Park in central Ohio on a Friday. It was unbearably hot and humid that afternoon, but at least the skies looked clear, and anyway, I knew we'd have lots and lots of trees at our group campsite to provide shade.

We checked in and drove slowly to our area, where we found—you guessed it—absolutely no trees to provide shade. Large, air-conditioned RVs had grabbed those spots well ahead of us; the campground was full. We had zero chance of changing locations.

We were the only stupid campers in sight.

As I stared out the window at brown, barren grass that had all the shade capacity of, say, Death Valley, Nevada, the Bob Walsh party waved as they drove quickly away in their air-conditioned SUV.

"We'll be at the lodge," yelled Bob. "Call us if you want! You guys have fun!"

Punks.

The remaining three sets of families parked cars and tumbled out into the wet, oppressive heat. Ninety-eight percent humidity. Several children, including two toddlers. One woman, my BFF Amber, pregnant and very nauseous. These sound like reasons *not* to camp, but lo, they were the circumstances. There were 11 of us—and one on the way.

This was going to be just a peck of rustic entertainment, I could tell.

But we went ahead and set up stupid camp. We unpacked our sleeping bags, inadequate shelter and warm bottled water. We sweated, we grunted, we groaned.

Have I mentioned there was no shade?

We began two days of rustic camping: not sleeping in beds, sweating, not flushing, sweating, drinking tepid bottled water, sweating, and trying to entertain several cranky children, who were sweating. The Hobo, age four at the time, soon developed a heat stroke, and tossed and turned with fever on the mattress of our 104-degree, Dutch-oven tent.

"I want to go home," he moaned.

It was time to do something. The 11 of us—and one on the way—piled into our respective vehicles, blasted the air conditioning and drove across the campground to the lodge. Here, we sat drooling in the parking lot, because lowly rustic campers like us were not permitted to use the fancy-pants resort facilities.

But we soon figured out how to solve that problem with a little creative storytelling, a.k.a. lying.

"We're with the Bob Walsh party! Room 209!"

And we hustled the children past lodge staff and lifeguards into the air conditioning, the indoor pool, the restroom. We swam. We relaxed in AC.

We flushed.

We spent an entire afternoon amongst such luxuries as roofs, ice cubes and functioning plumbing. Life was all rainbows and unicorns and running water when you were among the Bob Walsh party, Room 209.

Though we tried—hard—we couldn't loiter at the lodge and pretend to be Bob Walsh for the entire weekend.

So we drove dejectedly back to the stupid campsite, a.k.a. the Sahara, where we had one, and only one, thing going for us: a large, brand-new gazebo-type shade tent that I had just purchased the week before.

We set it up, tying three ends of it down with stakes, and one end to Jimmy Powell's Chevy Blazer for extra stability. We did just about everything under the gazebo that evening: cooked, sweated, ate, sweated, drank, sweated. Next, we pulled a picnic table underneath it, where my pregnant, nauseous BFF sat, pale as a ghost, with her head in her hands—and sweated.

"This really can't get much worse," she said. "I want to go home."

And that's when the storm blew in.

Lightening flashed. Thunder rumbled. Dark, foreboding, evil clouds roiled on the horizon, and my eyes traveled from the sky to our young kids to the woefully inadequate tents.

As the thunderstorm unleashed its initial fury, the 11 of us—and one on the way—huddled under the only shelter we had, which was, of course, the new shade gazebo we'd set up.

At that point, Jimmy Powell ran to his Blazer to wait out the storm. Or so we thought, until he started the engine.

"What the hell is he doing?" said Tony.

And I don't mean to name names here, but Jimmy Powell put his car into gear and Jimmy Powell lurched forward, yanking along with him our gazebo, our shade, our only adequate shelter for the entire weekend. The 11 of us—and one on the way—stood helplessly under the collapsing roof as he obliviously demolished it. We finally figured out that he was headed to the ice machine, and as we watched him drive away, dragging the big tent, its last remaining stake flew out of the ground and gashed me across the neck.

"I want to go home," I said, wiping away blood.

And that's about the last thing I remember from the stupid camping trip.

I learned many life lessons that weekend, many valuable, sweaty, bloody life lessons, such as the fact that canned beer makes a great bandage/ice pack, rustic camping really, truly sucks, and you should never tie anything to Jimmy Powell's Blazer.

Anything you want to keep, that is.

But far and away, the most important thing I learned from the Stupid Camping Trip of 2007?

Always, always, *always*—trust me on this one—say you're with the Bob Walsh party. Room 209.

CHAPTER TWENTY-EIGHT
Airplanes. Personal Space Is Just a Suggestion
Monday, 12:48 p.m.

I am not anti-social. I prefer to think of it as "selectively social."

Yet, despite my best efforts, people keep talking to me.

Just like today: I'm wearing headphones and staring intently at my phone. So clearly, I want to have a conversation.

"How you doin'?"

He's nudging my arm and leaning towards me. I can smell his lunch: nachos, beer, a little something in the way of garlic.

"Fine, thanks," I give him a half-smile but keep my eyes down, hoping to send a signal.

"Where you from?"

Signal FAIL.

"Columbus," I mumble.

"Yeah? I'm from Columbus, too!"

Shocking news, since we're on a flight from Atlanta to Columbus.

I pull off my earbuds and set them aside. He's tall, mid-40s, eagerly looking at me. I know the type; he won't be deterred. I seem to have the sort of demeanor and/or body language that invites conversations from strangers. Long, unsolicited, inane conversations from strangers.

The thing is, I really don't like chatting—at all. I will write emails, I will text, I'll Facebook you all night long, baby. But I don't want to communicate via voice, either on this phone, or in person. There are seven billion people on the planet. Of these, I enjoy actually physically talking with maybe, oh, five.

I'm not sure why, but I seem to have the opposite effect on others. I think people see my short stature and light hair-color and assume I have a friendly, bubbly personality.

This couldn't be further from the truth. I am quiet and actually kind of a bitch. Just ask my family.

Here on the plane, my seatmate's glassy eyes stare me down as he leans even closer, his saggy pants offering up a plunging rear view, a scandalous posterior eyeful I neither expect nor desire. Before my attempt to nap, I had noted that he carried no luggage, and this—along with his bloodshot eyes and visible crack—make him seem kind of gangsta.

Then again, I'm pretty gangsta myself, what with my huge purse and yoga pants.

Still, he seems a friendly fellow, an amiable hoodlum, and intent on talking to me no matter how much I'd rather sleep. Speaking of sleep, he has a request.

"Hey—if I nod off here, can you get me some of them pretzels and a Sprite when she comes by? I love them pretzels."

"Absolutely," I say. I'd hate to deny a guy his airplane snacks.

My new friend chatters on and on until I'm good and annoyed, and then eventually nods himself into a nap. As the flight levels off, I pass the time by playing Diner Dash, and when the stewardess comes past, as promised, I get Dr. Droopy Drawers his allotted 4 ounces of soda and tiny bag of pretzels. I nudge him in the arm. Hard.

"Oh! Thanks, ma'am." He opens his pretzels and begins munching.

Ma'am. He better watch out, using that word—he's well within striking distance. See sentence re: nudge above.

"So. What do you do for a living?" he asks.

"I work in communications," I reply. I've learned that it's best to be vague in these situations.

"Really? Where you work?"

"It's downtown," I dismiss it with a wave—again with the vague. "How about you? Where do you work?"

He pauses chewing, rubs his chin, smiles to himself and sits back.

I have a sudden feeling things could get intriguing.

"Well, there's this medicine—these pills . . ."

"Uh-huh." Oh, we're going to have fun here, I can tell.

"They're cracking down on them in Columbus, big time," he says.

"Really . . ." This conversation might be better than a nap. Maybe.

"The people—they're addicted to them. Bad. They're like . . . pills for pain, pills for pain," He looks at me, waiting for my reaction, his expression dancing a thin line between warning and sales pitch.

"Yeah. You're talking Percocet, Vicodin, OxyContin. Right?" I ask.

He's relieved that I'm familiar with such "pills for pain," I can tell because his shoulders relax. He leans toward me, and I smell nachos. Again.

"See, they're cracking down in them in Columbus. So what I do, I get on a plane . . . "

His voice a whisper, he leans even closer to me. I can now just about taste his lunch. And his beer. And his pretzels

But I'm suddenly very interested in what he has to say.

". . . I get on a plane, see, and I go to these . . . mom-and-pop places, down Florida? And I get 'em filled, these prescriptions, and I bring 'em back."

He leans back in his seat, clasps his hands. He's pleased with himself. You can tell.

Ah, yes. The glassy eyes, the lack of luggage—and several other things about this fella all click into place for me. I nod, I smile. And I remain quiet.

"So?" he asks. My silence has indicated that I'm definitely not in the market—for pills, anyway—and he changes the subject. "You married?"

"Yes."

"That's cool, that's cool," he says. "What's your husband do?"

And here it is folks.

"Well," I turn my head and look at him.

Wait for it, wait for it . . .

"He's a police officer."

My seatmate recoils, his rheumy eyes bulge and he jerks back in his chair as if I've shot him. "Oh—whoa! Whoa! Oh please, please. Oh man, oh man!" He buries his face in his palms, shakes his head back and forth.

Dawn - 1, Hoodlum - 0. I plug my headphones back in my ears and pick up my phone. Hey. What can I say?

I didn't choose the thug. The thug chose me.
Enjoy your pretzels, Sir Gangsta.
And remember: You really should be vaguer in these situations.

CHAPTER TWENTY-NINE
As Soon As You Remember Your Password, It's Time to Change Your Password
Tuesday, 6:44 a.m.

It's pouring rain—again. Traffic is ridiculous—again.

And I'm back in my cubicle, forced to wear pants.

Again.

It sure is Tuesday. The numbers in the corner of my cell phone here read 6:44 a.m., but already things seem pretty dismal, what with the rain, traffic and mandatory wearing of the pants.

Still, I need to clock in, so I collapse into the chair and ctrl-alt-delete into the computer. And that's when my day goes the rest of the way down the crapper:

"Please change your password. Your password will expire in one day, and you will not be able to log in."

Son of a *bitch*.

I should have known—I should have *known* it'd be time to change my password, because I had just finally remembered my current password. In fact, your modern corporate infrastructure technology manuals state, and I quote:

"As soon as staff members remember their current password, force them to create a new password. Mwa-ha-ha!"

I have no choice in the matter, so on the "Change Your Password" screen, I type in my old secret word in the proper field, and under "New Password," I type in a couple of numbers and the name of my childhood dog.

"Sorry, but you cannot use an old password."

Huh. Must have used that dog already. So I type in the name of another childhood dog.

"Sorry, but you cannot use an old password."

I'm running out of dead childhood dogs. Still, I type the name of a third deceased dog and click "OK."

"Sorry, but your password must contain an uppercase letter."

I type in a couple of numbers and the name of the third dog with a capital letter.

"Sorry, but your password must contain at least one uppercase letter and a symbol."

Oh, I have some uppercase letters and symbols for them. Several, in fact, and they go like this:

G@D*MM!T!!

I have to play nice, however, as I am fond of receiving paychecks and all, so I type in some numbers, the capitalized name of the third dead dog, and an asterisk sign.

"Sorry, but your password must contain at least one uppercase letter, a number, a symbol, Jimmy Hoffa's location, lyrics from a Rush song, and the blood of your firstborn child."

This password is also too weak. I quote again from the IT manual:

"Force staff members to create passwords with requirements that will make it impossible for them to remember said passwords. Mwa-ha-ha!"

After several attempts, I manage to power through and eventually give IT what they want, including—but not limited to—capital letters, my kid's DNA, GPS coordinates of mobster remains, lyrics from the *Moving Pictures* album, and finally, I receive the joyous news:

"Your password has been successfully changed!"

I've lost 15 minutes during this exercise in idiocy. It's time to get busy and log in to other very important, very work-related accounts, such as Facebook, Twitter and Pinterest, which require three completely different passwords, none of which I can remember.

Son of a *bitch*.

Even though it's a pain, I understand why security is so tight, why we need so many different passwords. I do. Hackers, spammers, denizens of several dusty, angry, third-world countries—they want to pilfer my identity and the number of my very valid, very American credit card. And all these bad guys seem very good at finding ways to figure out my password. In fact, the only person who seems incapable of guessing my password?

Me.

I began using the Internet in 1997. Some folks started utilizing it way earlier than that, however they're all from California, so they don't count. But my point—and I had one here, somewhere—is that I've been making up secret codes for dozens of different accounts for nigh on 16 years, and therefore my brain is just done with passwords. Full of passwords. Out of RAM for passwords. Except for one: my Yahoo email password, which has been the same since—you guessed it—1997. I keep the Yahoo account for three reasons:

1. I'm too lazy to delete it.

2. I can remember the password, because I've had it for nearly two decades.

3. It amuses me because the emails are chock-full of very good, awesome news!

It's true. Everybody on Yahoo wants to meet you. They email or IM you to say they'd like to have a chat, go on a date, get married; and they're always offering to give you things, such as Viagra samples, sexual favors, herpes, etc., etc.

Because Yahoo is the only password I can recall on this dismal Tuesday, I decide to log in and cheer myself up with a little fun, Viagra and herpes.

And that's when I find it, right here on my phone screen: wonderful, happy news from a "MR. PAUL ARUNA" of the "BANK OF AFRICA," who informs me in an email filled entirely with SHOUTY CAPITAL LETTERS that I have inherited 27.2 MILLION DOLLARS!

According to the email, it seems at one time that I had rich Kenyan relatives—five of them. But sadly, they passed away in a plane crash in 2003, leaving me the princely sum of 27.2 million dollars!

Read on for the letter from Mr. Aruna:

I WANT THE BANK TO RELEASE TO YOU THE MONEY AS THE NEXT OF KIN TO OUR DECEASED CUSTOMER.

I want the bank to release money to me also, Mr. Aruna. I am a big supporter of anyone who wants to release money to me.

I NEED YOUR URGENT ASSISTANCE!

How can I help?

I WANT TO TRANSFERRING THE SUM OF (USD $27.2 MILLION DOLLARS) TO YOUR ACCOUNT WITHIN 10 BANKING WORKING DAYS. THIS MONEY HAS BEEN DORMANT FOR YEARS IN OUR BANK WITHOUT ANY BODY CLAIMING THE FUND.

Absolutely. Let me take the money off your hands and be the body to claim the fund. How do I do so?

I NEED THE FOLLOWING INFORMATIONS: NAME, AGE, ADDRESS, SOCIAL SECURITY NUMBER, BANK, CHECKING ACCOUNT ROUTING NUMBER.

Well! This all sounds great, Mr. Aruna, it really does.

I LOOK FORWARD TO HEARING FROM YOU AND RECEIVING YOUR INFORMATIONS.

I bet you do! And I'd give you all of that INFORMATIONS from the bank website, I certainly would—but I just can't seem to remember the password.

Yeah. I don't think Mr. Aruna has my best interests at heart. Call me a genius, call me a pasty white girl, call me a fifth-generation American of German descent. But something tells me none of this is true: I don't have any rich Kenyan relatives, dead or otherwise.

So I guess I'll have to stay gainfully employed. Guess I'll have to keep making up passwords. Guess I'll have to continue to wear pants. Because no one one—Mr. Aruna included—really wants to give me millions of dollars. Lord knows I've asked around.

CHAPTER THIRTY
Apparently, Word of My Many Charms Has Spread to the Ukraine
Wednesday, 12:15 p.m.

It's not every day a girl gets a marriage proposal.

From another girl.

Here I am at the office, minding my own and playing Words With Friends on my break, when my cell phone pings with an international email. I don't often get such correspondence at work, and the last time I did, it contained news that I had inherited money from a rich relative in Kenya!

So of course I click it open immediately, but sadly, none of my rich Kenyan relatives has died. This letter comes from one Roksana Tsvetka, a young Ukrainian woman. Imagine my great surprise when she asks to be my wife and says she'll come live with me in the U.S.!

And I don't mean to brag, folks, but this proposal? Comes from royalty.

"I will be your Princess," she writes.

How do you like me now? She throws down more enticing news:

"I will take you to the Wonderland full of Harmony and Miracles!"

Harmony and Miracles? I could use some Harmony and Miracles! And what is this "Wonderland?"

Although Miss Tsvetka hasn't met me in person yet, she must have heard: Along with my average looks, she could have a piece of a very exhilarating American life, filled to the brim with many exciting activities! Such as shopping at Walmart! Driving with dummies in traffic! Sitting in a cubicle! Scooping up dog crap!

Evidently, Roksana wants to lead the glamorous life.

Unfortunately for her Highness, I am already married—to a man and stuff—and even if I wasn't married, it's dudes I dig. Although Harmony and Miracles are very tempting, I enjoy the Franks and Beans.

Not the Bikini Biscuit.

Still, the Princess paints a pretty picture. I thumb down through the email, and she teases me with her skills and assets:

"My major interest or I may call it hobby," she writes, "I admire to cook true Ukrainian dishes."

Hold the phone. She cooks? Do you mean, for example, that I could arrive home at 7 p.m. to find, like, actual food? For, like, me? Most days, all I encounter after work are dirty dishes and leftover frozen Tony's Pizza crusts—which I scarf down immediately.

You know, I am a fan of the old Thrill Drill. But I have to admit this gets more intriguing by the minute. I read on:

"I have been given birth in 1986," writes her Highness. "I have a blue eye and black hairs. I have height of 179 centimeters and a weight of 45 kilograms."

I can get past the one eye. But we'd have to work on her English skills. I know not these "centimeters" and "kilograms" of which she speaks.

Still, it's all very exciting. So I post the news of my unexpected proposal on mobile Facebook, and my notifications bar fires up like a Ukrainian red-light district. Thirty-some people, most of them female, are happy for me.

Oddly enough, very few male Facebookers comment on my exhilarating news. Do they not covet the Harmony, the Miracles, the Wonderland?

Every guy I've ever known wants to go to Wonderland *all* the dang time.

But the women—I think they like the idea of a wife.

My friend Kim, working mom and busy general manager of a Ford dealership, has this to say:

"Ladies, ladies, think about it. You walk in the door from a long day at work, your meal is on the table, your house is clean, your laundry is done, your kids have been picked up from all their activities and the grass is mowed! Heck yeah! It's Miller Time!"

Kim? You've really got something there. Dip sticks be damned—her Highness and I will just have an arrangement. I'm forty-damn-four. I am quite familiar with celibacy.

Because a clean house? Finished laundry? An actual meal? For actual me?

That's all the harmony and miracles I'll ever need, right there.

Yo. Princess Roksana . . .

Call me.

CHAPTER THIRTY-ONE
Workers of America: Your Cubicles Are Not Soundproof
Thursday, 6:29 a.m.

It's noisy, I feel miserable and I'm wearing clothing against my will. I must be at work.

Clothing is overrated, as is work. And really, I see no need to either:

1) Wear clothes; or,

2) Stay at work today. Or any day.

I suppose I should explain—it's not the actual *tasks* of my job I dislike. Also I'm fond of paychecks.

It's the workplace itself, the getting to and fro, along with the necessity for uncomfortable attire, that I find objectionable, and I'm trying to forget I'm here but . . .

Wheerrrr!

Sadly, I am at work, and I can tell because even though it's early and I haven't clocked in yet, the *Wheerrrr!* automatic paper towel dispenser has announced the day's first visitor to the *Wheerrrr!* kitchenette.

No one consulted me about this paper towel dispenser. If they had, I'd have chosen something else for drying purposes. Something quieter—such as a jet engine.

I'm so glad my cubicle is located right next to the kitchenette, where I hear *Wheerrrr!* and smell everything, everyone and the stinky crap they cook for lunch. I've sat here for so long that I can tell who is in the kitchen by their paper towel usage. That, my friends, is talent. Or slow-brewing insanity. Join me—won't you?—during an average morning at an average job in nearly Any City, USA.

Wheerrrr-Wheerrrr-Wheerrrr-Wheerrrr!

And here's Kathy, Worst Abuser of the Paper Towel Dispenser.

Hundreds, nay, thousands of trees have fallen in her name, so that she *Wheerrrr!* can line the microwave *Wheerrrr!* with nine layers of paper *Wheerrrr!*, as well as wash and dry her many, many dishes.

Day after day, Kathy shuffles in loaded down with Kroger bags and spreads her food out across the counter, blocking the microwave, the sink, the entire kitchenette. Next, she begins the 40-minute process of preparing her meal: wheat germ, protein powder, some kind of green, slimy milkshake. I see, in her wake, a week's worth of groceries.

She sees breakfast.

Wheerrrr!

Paper Towel Abuser/Tree Murderer isn't her only title. Kathy is also the World's Chubbiest Health Expert, just chock-full of nutrition and fitness advice. She wants to give you a daily dissertation on diet and exercise, because—although she's dieted for nine years and hasn't shed a pound—you're the one who's doing it wrong.

I need to go in there and get some breakfast, but I'm putting it off. Kathy's Morning Meal Prep and Wellness Expo generally runs more than an hour, and I'm aware of the protein content in my Greek yogurt; she's already given me the info—four times.

I think I'll just take a minute to sit here in my cubicle, do some Important Work Research on Facebook, try to relax so I can begin my day and . . .

"So I called the doctor. Remember that problem I was having, with my bowel movements?"

Ah, shit. TMI Todd has called his mom. Again. He'll proceed to have a loud personal phone conversation that will make me want to stab myself with a pen.

Yes, Todd, I'm sure your mom remembers the issue with your bowel movements, because you told her last week. Everyone in a five-cubicle radius remembers the issue with your bowel movements.

We will *never forget* the issue with your bowel movements.

I want to tell him this. I want to tell him several things all of which begin with "Keep it down, Todd!" and end with:

"You seem to have forgotten that our walls are one-inch thick and made of fabric."

"Yes. We can hear you, Todd. We can hear you breathing."

"And your loud personal phone conversations are interfering with our Facebooking."

Do I say any of these things? No, I am polite, so I say nothing, and TMI Todd launches into a 26-minute description of his colonoscopy.

Luckily, I've sat near him for a long time, and I've learned that it's best just to zone out when he loudly shares too damn much information.

I know what to do. I send my mind to its happy place: the couch—the couch at home. Because instead of sitting here at work, trussed up in pants and a bra and all manner of unpleasant clothing, I could be there, on the couch, at home.

Unlike here, I bet I could even get some work done at home; I have a laptop and Internet access. I am fancy like that.

And then it hits me: I really don't have to be at work. A great deal of my job *could* be done at home. Without paper towel machines. Or TMI Todd.

Or clothing.

People—think of the peace! Think of the solitude! Think of the potential for nakedness!

Yeah, I could just sit on the couch, lean my head back and . . .

"WELL, I MADE IT! TRAFFIC WAS TERRIBLE! I-70 IS DOWN TO ONE LANE!"

Traffic Jack. He's just arrived at the office, and he wants to let you—and everyone else in the tri-cubicle area—know. Stay tuned as Traffic Jack shouts the traffic report over-top the cubicle walls . . .

"I MEAN WHAT IS WRONG WITH PEOPLE? THEY DRIVE TOO FAST. THEY DRIVE TOO SLOW. NOBODY DRIVES RIGHT!"

I really shouldn't bother coming to work so early. I can't get anything done until the noise dies down at 9:30, after Todd gives TMI, Kathy winds up her Wellness Expo, Jack finishes his broadcast and . . .

Hack-hack-hacka-hack! *Snort*

. . . Next-Door Dick, the Open-Mouthed Cubicle Cougher has cleared his sinuses for the day. No, Dick does not bother covering his mouth when he coughs or sneezes; he has zero respect whatsoever for basic hygiene and disease prevention. Even though I can't see him, yes, I can tell his mouth is open. You could, too, if you were here.

So there you have it. I bet you recognized these folks, on an average morning at an average job in Any City, USA. That's right. Are you tired of sunlight, warm air and plant life? Bored of basic human privacy? Fond of tight, constricting clothing? Do you feel like dying a little inside, every day? Then join me! And Jack and Kathy and Dick and Todd and . . .

". . . the stuff they give you the night before the colonoscopy? That is some kind of poop juice, I tell you what. I was crapping out things I hadn't even eaten yet!"

Yes sir. Come on over. Bring your breakfast!

Wheerrrr!

CHAPTER THIRTY-TWO
If Your Clothes Fit, Be Suspicious. Be Very Suspicious
Friday, 5:20 p.m.

Sometimes, I pass by a mirror or a window and think, "OK—44 years old. Not bad . . . "

And other times I pass by my reflection and think, "Wow. Who is that elderly pregnant woman?"

Time marches on, and like most mid-lifers, I'm most certainly shuffling toward old age and obesity. Worse, in recent years, I have blown up like a poisoned dog. My already formidable stomach has bloated to epic proportions, though I'm not sure why, despite kitten-sized portions and OCD exercise habits.

But apparently the combination of middle age, a six-month Ohio winter and a ten-hour a day desk job have caught up with me. The scale reads new and alarming numbers normally associated with a woman double my height. Also, my stomach can't seem to let go of the fact that it housed children—twice—and I still have the big barrel-shaped gut to show for it.

Sometimes these same children catch a glimpse of this same naked belly, the one that lovingly carried and nurtured them, the one that writhed through torturous hours of agonizing labor to bring them into this world. When this happens, and the kids accidentally see me in a state of "underwear," their reactions are, well, far from reverent:

"Ewww! Gross!" says the Hobo.

"Mother! Put some clothes on!" says the Princess.

It's not their fault, really, that they continually remind me of my impending demise, my foot in the grave. Gravity and time have not pummeled their perfect little bodies yet, and they possess the smooth, flawless, muscle-packed skin that only the young can claim—and take for granted.

I, on the other hand, I resemble a pregnant Jabba the Hutt. Although I am most assuredly not pregnant now, judging by erratic visits from my monthly friend, and the fact that I'm experiencing many of the symptoms of perimenopause.

As you can imagine, all these things usually combine to put me in a bad mood.

But not today. It's going to be a great day. I can tell because my shirt fits.

That's a rare thing—currently, none of my shirts fit. None of my dresses fit. We will not speak of the pants. Shh. Hush now.

I could, of course, go and buy new clothing in a bigger size, but to me, that is admitting defeat and also makes too much sense.

I yank this particular top out of a dark closet just after 5 a.m. this morning, not caring, at that point, which one it is, what it looks like, not even caring whether it's mine. The only thing I'm concerned about at 5 a.m. is remaining upright. I pull the shirt over my head and marvel at its comfort, its looseness, its lack of boob and belly binding.

"Huh," I think. "Maybe I'm losing weight?"

Doubtful. And lately, I've grown used to tight, constricting clothing. I'm always at the Land of Uncomfortable Apparel, a.k.a. the office, anyway.

It's work. Everybody's miserable.

And it is time to get there, so I pull on some appropriately unpleasant pants and walk out the door.

While driving, I notice immediately that I can breathe—the blouse isn't squeezing my lungs in normal fashion. Downright intoxicating, it is, this newfound ability to inhale and exhale without restraint.

"Huh," I say to myself. "Maybe I really am losing weight?"

I park the car and walk past the slouching bums and crackheads to my building, enjoying the cool breeze under my billowy top. I ride the elevator to the 25th floor, and make the usual rounds: the coffee pot, the water cooler, the bathroom. Others notice my newfound svelteness.

"You look good!" they say.

"Thanks!" I reply.

"Are you losing weight?"

"Huh," I say. "I don't know. Maybe. Thanks!"

Glowing from the adulation of my many fans, I float back to my desk, where I fantasize that, perhaps one day, all my clothes will actually fit again. I'll break the futile cycle of tiny portions/endless exercise/stubborn scale, and be able to pick something—anything—from the closet and pull it on with ease. The children will once again see me in a state of "underwear," and have nothing but positive things to tell me:

"You look good, Mom!" they'll say.

"Thanks!" I'll reply.

"Are you losing weight, Mom?"

"Huh," I'll say. "I don't know. Maybe. Thanks!"

I feel downright giddy. I'm not used to being in a good mood at the office, see comment re: work = misery + uncomfortable clothing above.

But today, life is all sunshine and blue skies and shirts that fit.

Glancing down, I take a better look at the wondrous garment. It is peach, a stretchy cotton that flows down the length of the torso, landing on its own fabric folds—not the folds of my flesh.

"Huh," I say.

For sure, the shirt brings me comfort and joy.

But it is not without a problem, which is the itchy tag. Tags of any sort drive me nuts, irritating my skin and driving me to scratch myself raw, the bloody track marks resembling those of a heroin addict.

So I reach for the scissors, stretch the tag taut and snip.

And that's when I see it:

Old Navy

Old Navy. Cool. I should definitely stop and get more of these shirts.

Size - Medium

In medium. Not even a large!

Maternity

Maternity.

A-ha. Yes, well. That explains a lot.

CHAPTER THIRTY-THREE
The Best Pants Are No Pants
Tuesday, 6:56 a.m.

Shhh. Don't tell the boss, but my pants are really comfortable.

Odd, I know. One isn't supposed to feel this good at work; one is supposed to feel miserable here. As we've established, I'm not a fan of work, or pants, or anything that requires pants. I am, however, a fan of things that *don't* require work or pants, especially napping.

But I'm not very good at napping. I have been engaged in an increasingly futile attempt to nap since 1997, when my first child was born. All forms of sleep elude me these days, and the older I grow, the less I sleep, to the point where I don't think I will ever lie down long enough to die. I'll just stagger around for centuries—the planet's first certified zombie—a wild-eyed, hideous, rotten old woman, begging strangers for Ambien.

Mmm . . . Ambien.

Where was I? Oh yeah—my comfy pants. They were an accident.

Not long ago, I began looking for some straight-leg pants to go with my dozens of pairs of tall boots, and came across a black pair at a local close-out store. They had belt loops and little fake pockets, looked serviceable, nondescript, but still kind of fun and form-fitting. They treaded a thin line between marginally acceptable and wildly inappropriate.

In short, they were just like me.

I have always loved what I call a "two-fer"—a useful, entirely awesome item that pulls double duty. I felt that with the right tops at the right times, these slacks could easily serve dual purposes: Paired with a white cotton blouse, they said, "Fire up the laptop."

But with a lace shirt or a cami, they said "Have another margarita."

I took the pants into the store's dressing room. I wasn't sure they'd fit at first—they were a small size, a single-digit number I've long aspired to.

For years, I've been fighting that number; for years I've been fighting my pants. They strangle and crush my internal organs, puff my muffin-top, bloat me like a pregnant penguin—every breath I take is a battle with their fibers. Oh, sure, they look innocent enough in the closet: folded, behaving, pretending to fit. But I know the truth. I'll pull them on, and they'll cut me in half, gripping my gut like a vice.

I'm not sure why my pants hate me so; I've been good to them. I painstakingly follow care labels ("Machine Wash Cold. Hang Over Treadmill to Dry") so that they air out slowly, allowing for maximum butt and belly stretch. But still, they taunt me with their tightness, depressing me, bringing me down, forcing me to cope with high-end pharmaceuticals, such as Miller Lite.

If I had my way, I'd go without pants. Pesky societal norms.

I thought about all this that day in the dressing room, as I stood and stared at the low-priced lovelies. "Well, here goes nothin'," I said, and I shrugged and pulled them up.

They slid over my hips like butter. Luscious, luscious butter.

It had to be a mistake. No yanking and pulling, no sweating and cussing to get them on? And the material—oh, the material! It felt soft, it felt yielding, it felt downright stretchy.

It also felt familiar, so I looked at the label, which read "70 percent Lycra." That, I knew, was the same percentage of Lycra as my favorite yoga pants. These pants were yoga pants in a work-pants package. These, my friends, were glorified sweat pants. These pants were exactly $6.

I was falling in love. With pants.

Oh, yes. For that price, they would be mine—all mine. I took them off, put my old, uncomfortable, entirely inferior pants back on, walked out of the dressing room and threw the new bottoms into the cart. I rushed back to the clearance rack with the intent of buying them in every color, but alas—the black pair was the last pair.

I happily paid for my $6 lovelies and took them home. The next morning, I paired them with some boots and a white cotton blouse, then walked out into the kitchen to grab my things and leave for work.

"Nice jeggings," said my daughter, coming up the stairs from the basement.

Jeggings?!

"*Jeggings*?!" I yelled, flabbergasted. "These are *not* jeggings! They're just . . . pants. Comfortable pants. Six-dollar pants!"

"Sure they are," she walked over and yanked at the fabric. "Stretchy, straight legs, fake pockets. Those are definitely jeggings."

Jeans plus leggings equals jeggings. Or so she'd told me, and nobody laughed harder than I did when I first heard the word. Oh yes. I laughed, I snorted, I rolled my eyes and scoffed. Although up to this point I'd never seen them, the whole concept sounded trashy and laughable and just so very . . . peopleofwalmart.com.

And now, here I am, the accidental owner of jeggings.

But I still don't like the name. We shouldn't call them jeggings. We shouldn't even call them "pants."

We should call them "no-pants."

Because that's what they feel like. They feel like sweat pants. They feel like yoga pants. They feel like no-pants. No-pants that aren't trying to kill me. No-pants so soft and stretchy, I forget they're there. No-pants that I can wear here in my cubicle, where I am comfortable enough to seriously consider taking a nap before I even clock in.

Mmm . . . no-pants napping at work. Now that's an idea whose time has come.

CHAPTER THIRTY-FOUR
Bad Day at Work? A Staff Meeting Will Ruin It Completely
Friday, 5:35 p.m.

Staff meetings: Yes, you can sleep with your eyes open.

Each week, I hope, I dream, I pray for redemption. Emailed, spoken, tapped out in Morse code—I'm not picky. I don't care. Three words, that's all I want:

"Staff Meeting Canceled"

Alas. It is not to be.

All-staff meetings, committee meetings, meetings to schedule meetings . . . in an ongoing quest to completely waste everyone's time, management continues to schedule these things constantly and worse—on Fridays.

I really don't work on Fridays. I show up. That's quite enough.

I've worked at several corporations over the last 20 years, and I've come to the conclusion that all staff meetings are basically the same. Calendar notifications pop up, and in a scenario repeated all across the U.S., workers stagger out of cubicles and into the conference room, their fates sealed.

You jockey for position around the table. Chair choice is crucial here: One must seek out a seat that's perfectly positioned to allow for surreptitious dozing and maximum hiding of one's smartphone. Facebook, Pinterest, Words With Friends—these are your allies in the staff meeting.

You plop down, and immediately begin to ponder very work-related, results-driven issues such as:

1. *How long will this fucking meeting last?*

2. *I hate wearing fucking pants.*

3. *How much longer until I can take off these fucking pants?*

Your best bet is to pretend to take notes during meetings. This allows you to pretend to be engaged and pretend to be awake.

You can also pretend to listen, as management discusses pointless concepts using ridiculous words that nobody understands. Consider these important notes I've collected over the years from many meetings at many jobs, along with their handy translations:

"We're going to re-vamp our *best practices*! (You'll be required to learn a shit-load of new rules, regulations and procedures that make absolutely no sense.)

"We've been discussing our *bottom line.*" (Somebody is getting laid off.)

"We need to change our *mindset*!" (You'll be changing job descriptions.)

"As part of our new direction, we will *leverage our assets.*" (Somebody's getting laid off.)

"We need to improve our *customer service.*" (You'll be working later and longer hours, with no change in pay.)

"Let's *think outside the box*!" (Let's waste countless hours to come up with wacky ideas that we'll never implement.)

"JoAnne has been very *pro-active* with the new processes." (JoAnne is a total ass-kisser.)

"We're going to play *hard ball* with our budget this fiscal year." (Somebody's getting laid off.)

"Our new customer service module *synergizes* with our core values." (Nobody fucking knows what synergize means.)

After this riveting discussion of the hard ball, the best practices, the impending layoffs, it's time for the boss to ask:

"Does anyone have any questions? Does anyone have anything to add?"

Silence! No questions! No! Everyone knows that at this point, keeping the mouth shut is the key to freedom and getting the hell out of there, to going home and removing the pants.

Everyone knows, that is, except pro-active JoAnne, who will perpetuate the agony by offering her input.

You would like to punch her.

Join us again next Friday, when we'll meet once more to discuss our *knowledge base* and revisit our *game plan*.

It will still be a bunch of *bullshit*.

CHAPTER THIRTY-FIVE
Hiding the Evidence: It's a Youngstown Thing
Tuesday, 5:32 p.m.

I borrowed his umbrella, broke it, then stuffed it back in his drawer. I figured he wouldn't notice.

My buddy Al—it was his umbrella. Al is my co-worker, a 6'4" black man. I am a 5'2" pasty white woman.

We are practically twins.

But Al is also burly and muscular, very capable-looking, a graphic designer with artsy retro-glasses and close-cropped hair. His look says either, "I can design you a logo," or "I can kick your ass," depending on his mood.

Though we work in Columbus, we both hail from greater Youngstown, Ohio, and we are of the opinion that this makes us savvier—and maybe a little tougher—than most folks. On our breaks, we like to discuss Youngstown Things.

Youngstown Things are shortcuts in your day, little life-hacks of possessions, methods, even attitudes, that can make a difference in your environment and your bank account. Here are some Youngstown Things my buddy Al and I recommend:

Windshield cracked, muffler hanging, water heater leaking? Duct tape: It's a Youngstown Thing.

Having major surgery? Worried about medical costs? There's really no need for anesthesia. Simply chug a 40-ounce in the hospital parking lot right before your appointment. Alcohol as anesthesia: That's a Youngstown Thing.

Stuck in traffic near an exit? Switch lanes and pass everyone on the right, then squeeze back over. You'll piss off some folks, but guess what? You're

I Love You. Now Go Away

almost home, they're still in traffic. Passing dummies on the right: totally a Youngstown Thing.

As you can see, our shared background, nearly identical looks and great love of Youngstown Things have made Al and me fast friends.

Years ago, on a rainy evening at quitting time, he heard me cussing, and although swearing at work is not uncommon for me, he asked what was wrong.

"I forgot my umbrella," I said, "and it's pouring outside."

"Come over here," he replied.

Al is not to be disobeyed; see info re: big and burly, above. I walked to his cubicle.

He pulled open his file cabinet. "There's an umbrella in here. You can borrow it any time."

And so I did. Borrowed it that night, the next night, and many other rainy nights over the next several years.

Yeah, I own an umbrella. But if I'm at work, it's in the car—six blocks away, and if I'm in the car, it's at my desk. I always know where my umbrella is: My umbrella is wherever I'm not.

The last time I borrowed Al's umbrella, a few weeks ago, it was raining sideways. No such thing as sideways rain, you say? It's Ohio. It rains however the hell it wants, and often. On this particular evening, the wind kicked up, in a sideways fashion, and blew My Buddy Al's umbrella inside out, busting the hinges. Broke it beyond repair.

Soaking wet, I hunched my way through the rest of the trek to the car, where I climbed in and threw Al's now useless umbrella into my backseat. Then, before he arrived at work the next day, I snuck over to his file cabinet and slid its mangled, lifeless body back into the drawer.

Do not judge me. He never used the umbrella, so I didn't think he'd discover it anytime soon.

Covering your tracks: It's a Youngstown Thing.

No, I didn't feel guilty—just a bit nervous. The man is mostly a gentle giant, however, if he's in a certain mood, Al has been known to pelt me with stress balls.

Hours, days, weeks went by; he said nothing. Until just now, when I heard him grumble.

"Come over here."

Oh, I am busted. I can tell by his voice. But Al is not to be disobeyed, so I walk from my desk to his. There it is, the evidence, right in his lap.

"You broke my umbrella."

"Yeah," I reply, sheepishly. "Sorry about that, Al. It was really windy, you remember that one day? A couple weeks ago?"

"I can't believe you broke my umbrella, and didn't even tell me," he shakes his head, looking down at the tangle of metal and nylon in his lap.

"Yeah. Sorry, Al . . . "

With his head tilted like this, I can't read his expression, but he makes his disappointment very clear. I hear our co-workers giggling through the thin cubicle walls.

I return to my desk to await my stress-ball pelting, and sitting there, I think long and hard about my actions. I should have come clean about the crime, should have told him I ruined his umbrella after he's been so nice, lending it to me all these years. At the very least, I really should have told him and then bought him a new one.

Ah, but I didn't.

The afternoon wears on, and Al doesn't come pester me at my desk in his normal fashion. I figure he's pretty mad, and probably devising my punishment—one that involves stress balls.

Around 4:30, he calls to me again. "Come over here." I brace myself. I surely don't want to go. But Al is not to be disobeyed, and I report to his cubicle for my pelting.

"Made you something," he grumbles, and hands me what appears to be left of his umbrella. He's removed the pole, disassembled the ribs and cut a hole in the top. I hold it up.

"It's a poncho," he says. "Now you won't get wet in the rain, since you never have your umbrella."

I poke my head through the top and pull it on. True enough, I look like some fool in a poncho. I certainly won't get wet in the rain.

I learned a lot today, mostly that I should always fess up to my office crimes.

But I also learned that sometimes you'll break someone's umbrella, neglect to tell them, stuff it back in their drawer, and they will turn right around and make you a poncho.

And that? Is definitely a Youngstown Thing.

CHAPTER THIRTY-SIX
The BMV. No Pants Required
Monday, 3:18 p.m.

I had always thought of myself as a bit of a gangsta. It was evident by my mom jeans, sensible shoes and attendance at several major country music festivals.

Turns out, I was right. I *am* a gangsta. I am, in fact, a straight-up thug.

It all started the other day, when I learned that I needed to drive to beautiful downtown Canton, Ohio for a meeting the following week. So I filled out the corporate pool-car form, the way I've done a hundred times before. I gave them my birthdate, license number, maiden name, several pints of blood, first-born child, etc., etc., and clicked "send."

Then I went about my workday, completely unaware that I was a wanted criminal.

Later, I returned to my desk from my buddy Al's cubicle, where we had been discussing—on our break, of course—Important Work-Related Topics such as Youngstown Things, Reese's cups and the Aerosmith *Greatest Hits* album, when I saw the email:

Request Denied.

"Dear applicant: We're sorry. Your pool car request has been denied because your driver's license appears to be expired."

What? Surely this was a mistake, and it wasn't that I forgot to renew my license—I could swear I just got the thing. Four years gone by already? Come on. Clear as day, I remembered driving to the BMV and spending several hours of my life—hours, mind you, that I'll never get back—waiting in line. A very long, long line.

With trepidation, I grabbed my purse, unzipped it and slid my ID out of its pocket. My eyes traveled down the card:

Eyes: BRO

Hair: BLN

Weight: (The, um, "same" since 1995. And none of your damn business.)

Issued: 4-17-2009 Expires: 4-22-2013

Well, shit. Apparently, time flies when you're having no fun at all.

Here it was three weeks after my license's expiration, and I had no idea I had become a felon. Just driving around without a valid driver's license, like a crackhead. Fa-la-la.

I picked up the phone and thumbed over to Facebook, where I posted my criminal status. Everyone was extremely compassionate:

"Be afraid. Be very afraid," commented Heidi.

"You forgot to renew? Well, the memory is the first to go!" wrote Gaynell.

"Be prepared to pay the $20 fine!" said Kim.

"And don't forget the vision and hearing tests!" added Susan.

So supportive, these people. With friends like that, who needs BMVs?

I decided to call the husband for some help. As a policeman and all-around OCD paperwork/forms guy, he normally keeps me abreast of my expiring licenses and tags. It was time to tell the cop that his wife was a criminal, in a calm, kind, rational manner.

"Nice work, Sherlock!" I yelled over the phone. "You didn't tell me my license was going to expire!"

"Yeah," he said. "Whose license is it, exactly?"

"Can't you do this for me, the way you do my auto tags?" I asked.

"Again, I say—whose license is it, exactly?"

He wasn't being very helpful, so I hung up. I felt pretty bummed about losing the old card, because in 28 years of driving, my expired thug-license featured the only ID picture that I've ever liked: I actually looked nice in the photo, with few wrinkles and only one of my several chins showing.

The worst of it wasn't the loss of the good picture, or that my license had expired, or even the impending long, long BMV line.

No, the worst news of all was that I would have to fix my hair, apply makeup and wear pants on Monday.

As I've mentioned, I'm off on Mondays, and I hate pants. I'll happily don chinos or mom-jeans on my work-days, Tuesday through Friday, but on Monday, makeup, hair and pants are not part of my routine. In general, I loaf around my empty home with zero makeup and bed-head. Frankly, showering is just an option, one I make if I work out, and working out? Also just an option. And as for clothes on my day off, it's pajamas in the fall/winter and a swimsuit in the spring/summer.

Mondays at home: No pants required.

But there was no getting around it. I had to drive to Beautiful

Downtown Canton the following week, and for this, I needed a valid license. I'd have to fix my hair. I'd have to apply makeup.

I'd have to wear pants.

Or so I thought. More supportive Facebook friends—males, not surprisingly—chimed in and helpfully pointed out that I didn't really need to wear pants at the BMV.

"You will not stand out at the license bureau," said David.

"They only take pictures from the shoulders up," wrote Eric. "No need for pants."

These were valid points.

This morning, the Monday in question, I rolled out of bed and reluctantly showered. I blow-dried and styled my hair, and applied a full-face of makeup, cussing all the while.

But I might as well not even have bothered, as I stepped out into a hot, miserable, extremely humid day. My hair fell flat, and I promptly sweated off all my carefully applied makeup.

Still, I arrived at the license bureau to find an amazingly short line. I chatted up the clerk, did the tests and filled out the form.

Eyes: BRO

Hair: BLN

Weight: (The, um, "same" since 1995. And still none of your damn business.)

I left with a new license, complete with crappy picture, in 12 minutes flat, and I did not get charged a fine.

I also did not wear pants. Are you kidding me? It was 81 degrees with 92 percent humidity.

I wore shorts.

CHAPTER THIRTY-SEVEN
The Golden Rule: Don't Be a Jerk
Friday, 12:11 p.m.

We have a big problem, here in the office.

We should put together a plan, a committee—perhaps a massive, alarming report to address what has become a major crisis for those of us on this floor.

You heard me. Alert the press! Call the authorities! At the very least, set up a freaking nanny cam! Because . . .

Someone in this office is not refilling the coffee pot!

Someone in this office is kind of a jerk!

Or maybe they just can't read, I don't know, as I personally put up a helpful sign in the kitchenette that reads:

"If you drink the last of the coffee, please make more."

I also politely added:

"Thank you."

Yeah—I'll admit it. I am the self-proclaimed Coffee Cop around here. Somebody had to take charge a while back, as non-coffee-makers were running rampant among us, pouring their coffee and then leaving the pot empty for the next person to make—time after time.

Despite my helpful sign, someone is doing it—or rather *not* doing it—again.

A few years ago, about 13 of us chipped in $10 each to buy a good coffee pot so we could avoid paying upwards of $5 per cup of Starbucks Mucho-Venti-Grande.

You can get about eight cups from one pot, and we, the 13, know the rules: Always ensure there is enough coffee for the next guy. Don't be a jerk.

It is just common coffee courtesy, and really should be written in the manual:

1. Make the coffee so there is some for the next guy.

2. Don't be a jerk.

I am the first one in the office every morning. As Chief Coffee Cop, I consider it my responsibility—nay, my civic duty—to plug the machine in, turn it on and make the coffee the way God and nature intended.

And so I do. I fill 'er up, plug 'er in, etc., etc., and make the coffee; then, I grab my full mug and head back to my soul-sucking cubicle.

A couple hours later, I head back into the kitchenette for another cup of coffee, where I find the pot empty.

"Jerks!" I say.

The swearing continues as I refill the pot, shovel grounds into the filter and wait, wait, wait for it to brew. It finishes, finally; I pour a cup and head back to my desk.

I stay there until mid-afternoon, when the caffeine buzz wears off, the carbs from lunch kick in, and I'm trying not to nod off at my desk. I grab my mug and head back into the kitchenette where I find—you guessed it— an empty coffee pot.

Cold. Bereft. Alone.

Again.

My co-worker and fellow Coffee Cop Mark and I are very concerned about this heinous crime, and we are on the case. We have been staking out the area, and we don't suspect the 13 original members of the coffee club. No, we suspect the Interlopers.

The Interlopers are a sorry group of folks who didn't fork over the $10, who felt they were above paying for the use of the machine. Oh yes—we, the Coffee Cops, have seen it with our very own eyes, these hooligans slipping into the kitchenette when they think no one is watching.

They grab the carafe, pour the last of the coffee, snatch their mugs and hightail it out the door leaving in their wake a cloud of dust and an empty coffee pot.

This afternoon, I'm sitting here on my break doing very productive things, such as checking Pinterest on my cell, when Mark stomps in, eyes blazing. "It's happening again. This has to stop!"

"I know," I say. "It's getting really bad."

Mark shakes his head in disbelief. "Seriously. What is wrong with people?"

"I have no idea," I tell him. "Are they blind? Are they stupid? Do they not see my helpful sign?"

"There's also a button," adds Mark. "A red button that says refill. They just . . . ignore it! Like it's not even there!"

"I know who it is, too."

"Me too. It's . . ."

We proceed to list the offending parties. In the interest of keeping our day jobs, I won't name them here.

But we discuss it at length, and we decide that The Interlopers are not just at work—they're everywhere, and they're easy to spot, because they go about their day not following the rules and rudely disregarding the most basic tenets of modern civilization.

They don't replace the toilet paper. They don't scoop their dog's poop. They don't let fellow motorists merge onto the freeway. They don't care when their cart blocks the entire canned goods aisle.

And they never—under any circumstances—ever make more coffee.

Personally, I dream of a world without Interlopers. I dream of a world with a full TP spool, and a sidewalk empty of dog poop. I dream of a world where I can merge freely onto the Interstate, and pick up a can of beans without the threat of a fist fight.

I dream of a world with a full coffee pot.

These are big dreams, I know.

But I believe they're possible if folks would simply have some courtesy. If they'd step back, be kind and read my helpful signs.

And all they really have to do is follow this simple, timeless, fundamental Golden Rule:

Don't be a jerk.

You see—you can't hide, Interlopers. We know who you are. The Coffee Cops are watching you, along with the nanny cam, God—and probably Mister Rogers.

And we are all very disappointed.

CHAPTER THIRTY-EIGHT
Lean Cuisine: Don't Tease Me If You Ain't Gonna Please Me
Tuesday, 12:02 p.m.

It looks pretty big.

From a distance, anyway. A good-sized package, appears hot and steamy, it should satisfy. It's supposed to be enough. That's what all the magazine articles say.

You draw closer, peering, tentatively touching it. Feels solid. However, after pulling off the covers, you're not sure it will do. There's really not much here. You can tell this whole thing will be over in two or three minutes.

But it's all you have. So you get it ready, warm it up. You close your eyes, open your mouth, place it on your tongue and then . . .

Blahhh!

Having a miniature frozen meal for lunch again today? Please. Try and contain your excitement.

Join the club. Around noon each day, all across the U.S., we, the working stiffs, stagger out of our cubicles and line up at the microwave with our sad little meals.

Lunch: This too shall suck

I can't help thinking that I get duped every time I bring one of these things to work. I mean, the marketing—so sexy! Oh, little box, you minx. How you taunt with your shiny packaging. Your "Mezzaluna Melt" from the "Cook's Collection." Like god-dang "Fine Dining!"

The impressive advertising fools me every time, I admit it. There are dozens of tiny options in my grocer's freezer, and I've tried most. They're

119

all the same, though they go by many names. The husband calls them "European portions." My college friend Robin dubbed them "starvation in a box." I just call them Budget Barf.

At least it's ample food. For a toddler.

Maybe.

Sure as hell isn't enough for me. I am a 5'2," small-framed female, but my mouth did not receive this memo, because I have the appetite of a professional Sumo wrestler. I don't get hungry. I get fungry: fucking hungry.

You wouldn't like me when I'm fungry.

And let me tell you something else. Just like Joey "How you doin'?" Tribbiani on *Friends*, I don't share food. Ever. Anyone attempting to split my grub will draw back a bloody hand. With a protruding knife. I will cut a bitch who wants "a bite."

I know, I know. I shouldn't stab people or eat that way, I should eat like the French do. French women eat small portions. French women savor their food. French women are thin and gorgeous. Blah, blah, blah— whatever.

French women suck.

I am an American girl of German lineage, raised near Youngstown around a bunch of Italians. I need some portions, yo. Some potatoes. A big plate of pasta. Or, better still, carbs with a side of carbs. Ladies and gents, I present to you—gnocchi: pasta made *of* potatoes. Gnocchi is Italian for "bring on the insulin."

So join me in my cubicle for lunch, but remember—bring your own pasta/potatoes, because Dawn (and Joey) don't share. We'll have gnocchi! We'll have a nap! We'll have a diabetic coma!

And those sexy packages? The Budget Barf? The European portions? Dead to us. You heard me, little box. Don't tease us if you ain't gonna please us.

Pitch

Thunk

Circular file.

Yeah. Shit just got real.

CHAPTER THIRTY-NINE
Minimum Wage Jobs: They're a Gas
Wednesday, 6:45 a.m.

As much as I grouse about putting on pants and a bra, driving to the office and sitting in my cubicle every day, there were times I worked much harder for far less pay.

Far, far, *far* less pay.

I refer to these times as the 80s. Also part of the 90s. And maybe 2003-2004.

Shut up.

I've flipped burgers. I've fried french fries. I've sold hardware. I've stocked shelves and filled salt shakers and waited tables and dealt with all manner of rude, impatient assholes. This for the staggeringly high rate of $3.35 an hour. And we are talking many hours.

Many, many, *many* hours.

One of these jobs, however, was different. One of these jobs was kind of fun. One of these jobs was pumping gas.

It had been a childhood dream of mine, pumping gas. As a kid, I watched with great anticipation as the men slouched out of the service station, grumbled, "How much?" and began filling the tank. Then, they pulled a squeegee from a bucket, dragged it across our windows, and wiped the excess with a paper towel. This process made me grit my teeth with joy.

(I know.)

(Shut up.)

Almost as thrilling as the squeegee were the coveralls the workers wore. Oh, the coveralls! A more serviceable garment I couldn't imagine, and plus they served as a "two-fer:" a useful item that fulfills two needs in one package. Shirt plus pants equals coveralls. I ask you, what could be better?

Only the squeegee.

I can hear you youngsters out there saying, "You're weird," and "I pump my own gas."

But, young grasshoppers, I assure you—it wasn't always this way. Back in the day, someone at the service station filled your tank as you sat in a warm car and watched.

These were times of women's lib and Gloria Steinem and "I Am Woman, Hear Me Roar." I was only five, but plenty old enough to notice that only males worked at these stations.

"Hey, Mom," I asked one day during a fill-up. "Do you think I could get a job pumping gas someday?"

For reasons I didn't understand, she stifled a smile.

"You can work anywhere you want to—women can do anything men can do," She paused for a minute, and then raised her brow. "Just make sure you finish college."

Sixteen years later, thanks to the hard work of Ms. Steinem, my mother, et.al, women certainly could work almost anywhere men could, albeit for less pay.

Far, far, *far* less pay.

Nonetheless, at age 21, I finally got my chance to work at a gas station.

I had three—count 'em, three—crappy minimum wage jobs that summer, all of which I needed because I'd engaged in the proud American tradition of maxing out the credit cards they gave like candy to university students. I'd used the money on important things, such as rent, textbooks and pitchers of beer.

Each of my jobs had a purpose: one for the Visa, one for the Discover and one for another Discover card that was mine but had my name spelled wrong. I used it anyway.

Job number three, for Discover card two, was at a Canfield, Ohio service station. Chuck the Manager hired me; he was a blonde, tan, perfect-looking Ken-doll of a guy who seemed better suited to Harvard or Yale than slinging cigarettes, bad coffee and watery gasoline on the outskirts of Youngstown.

"It's a pretty easy gig," he said, handing me a bright blue pair of coveralls.

His face turned serious. "Two rules: Always wear your coveralls. Keep them all the way on, over-top your street clothes, even if it's hot."

Considering my secret love of the garment, I didn't think this would be a problem. I nodded and waited for the second rule.

"And when you work full-serve, when you're the one who pumps gas, for God's sake, don't be in the bathroom!"

Poop before you pump. Got it.

I trained alongside seasoned service station veterans, such as my BFF

Amber, our friend Scott and various other characters, including a hilarious gay black man whose name I can't recall. Each shift, we either rang the register or worked full-serve.

I preferred full-serve, of course, as it mostly involved sitting around. It also meant that I could engage in my lifelong goals of pumping gas, wearing coveralls and using the squeegee.

Out at the pumps, you'd have your nice customers:

"Well hello, gorgeous!"

Your nice-but-maybe-a-little-sexist customers:

"Shouldn't you be working in a clothing store? At the mall?"

And of course, you'd have assholes.

"What took you so long? Jesus! Fill 'er up!"

You'd always have assholes.

But the hilarious gay black man whose name I can't recall knew how to deal with them.

"Yes sir!" he said.

Then, he pleasantly filled their tank, and waited until the car pulled from the pumps and out of earshot. He grinned as they watched him suspiciously in their rearview mirror.

"Asshole!" he'd hiss, smile and wave as they drove away. "That's right. Git on *outta here!*"

Inside the store, Chuck the Manager was not always around. This proved to be convenient, especially on the evening shifts I often worked, and his absence made for some pretty memorable nights at the Canfield gas station, nights in which we may or may not have engaged in such business friendly tasks as:

Splitting six-packs of Milwaukee's Best, kept hidden under the counter and poured surreptitiously into Styrofoam gas station coffee cups.

Blasting ZZ Top from a boom box turned up so high that we couldn't hear the customers on the other side of the kiosk, though we nodded and smiled and pretended we could.

Using the giant stick designed for changing gas price sign numbers to raise and lower in front of cars, thereby "directing traffic" in and out of the parking lot, toll-booth style.

Inviting our non-employee friends to hang out with us in the store, and sharing with them our music/beer/traffic-directing activities.

Chuck was either unaware of or turned a blind eye to our late-night shenanigans. He seemed an amiable Ken doll. But he meant what he said about pooping before pumping. Woe to the full-serve employee caught on the can.

"HEY!"

. . . came Chuck's yell, as well as his fist pounding on the bathroom door.

"C'mon! Pinch it *off* in there! Ya got a *full serve waiting!*"

I spent several educational, mischievous, constipated summer weeks working there at the gas station. Oddly enough, it was the coveralls that ended my promising career.

One humid, sweltering day, I'd stayed late to finish cigarette inventory. Because my shift was over, I'd unzipped my coveralls partway to cool off, exposing my t-shirt underneath, and of course, that's when the northeast Ohio regional manager showed up unannounced.

Of course it was.

"Your coveralls are supposed to stay *zipped up!*" he shouted. "At *all times!!*"

Balding, red-faced, all of 5'4," the pint-sized, middle-aged maniac waved his arms, stomping, raving and screaming at a schoolgirl.

"Relax! I'm off the clock!" I yelled back.

I quit before I could get fired, but I stayed for the show, watching this idiot with amusement as he stormed—still red-faced, still screaming—out the door and into his car.

"Asshole!" I hissed. "That's right. Git on *outta here!*"

Though I left the gas station for good that day, I learned many things in my short stint:

1. I definitely needed to finish college.
2. Styrofoam coffee cups have several uses.
3. In work, as in life, there will always be assholes.

Really, I didn't mind losing the gas station gig. I still had two other crappy jobs for the rest of the summer. And at least I had realized my childhood dream of pumping gas.

I dream big.

(I know.)

(Shut up.)

CHAPTER FORTY
Why So Cross, Crackhead?
Tuesday, 5:37 p.m.

I don't require much out of life. Most days, I just want to go home and remove my bra.

It's good to have goals.

Understand: I don't want to take it off for any kind of recreational purposes. What do you think this is? 2002? The 80s?

No, simply because by the end of each day, this damn hooter holster strangles my ribs, squeezes my heart and smashes my sandbags. Flat.

My bra is an asshole. I'm pretty sure it's trying to kill me.

Lots of things these days attempt to kill me, especially in the city, where I work. I could actually write several chapters on vehicles ("VW Beetle Catches Fire on I-70—Burns Short White Woman!") random building parts ("800-lb Balcony Railing Falls From the Tenth Floor—Smashes Short White Woman!") and other urban events that have all taken a good shot at me. Lately, it's the drunken crackhead thugs coming after me.

I have got to stop making eye contact with these people. Somehow I don't think they have my best interests at heart.

It's a small-town thing, the eye contact. As I've mentioned, I live in Brownsville, Ohio, and I'm originally from New Springfield, Ohio, a tiny burgh on the outskirts of Youngstown. Both my hometowns have a combined population of about 60, and I know all 60 of these people, their kids, their grandparents, their dogs and probably their dogs' grandparents. There, you greet folks, smile, usually exchange hugs. And it always helps to make eye contact with someone before you affectionately assault them.

Not so the crackheads here in Columbus. Best not to hug them. Best not to even look at them.

125

I've worked downtown eight years now, dutifully mastering my ear-buds-in-ears, eyes-on-the-phone technique. Have to. If I don't, the thugs stumble up to me. They ask for money. They ask for food. They ask me out.

I'm not in Brownsville anymore, apparently.

Somehow the crackheads sense the rural in me, the "nice girl," and they use that to hit me up for cash and meals and dates. So over the years, I've learned to spot them before they spot me.

I especially enjoy watching them from afar as I walk to work in the early morning. Stumbling to the YMCA after a hard night of partying, they've got their pants on the ground, underwear sagging. They weave down the sidewalk, wave their arms and mutter angrily—to no one.

Sometimes I wonder: Why, drunken crackhead, why so cross? You're headed for a day of leisure and sleep at the Y. I'm the one who has to put on a bra, wear pants, go to work. I'm the one who should be muttering angrily.

Great. Now I sound like a Republican, don't I? This is what the crackheads do to me.

Tonight, tired after a ten-hour workday, I'm off my game and not paying attention, staring down here at my phone while waiting for the light to change at the corner of Spring and High streets. I smell him before I see him. A mix of sweat and dirty hair and oozing-from-the-pores alcoholic stink. Odd for him to be out so early in the evening; the downtown thugs usually sleep it off until nightfall then start all over again—much like your average college student.

But here he is, right at rush hour, pasty-white and filthy and reeling toward the office drones as we wait to hop in our cars, go home, remove our bras.

I know the drill. I keep my eyes down, on my phone, and turn up the music. I have the look. The look that says, "Step off, thug! I know all about your shifty ways!"

He walks right up to me—of course he does.

I tell you, I am a God-dang crackhead magnet.

And he gets all up in my personal dance space, inches away, exhaling his flammable stink near my nose. I clutch my purse in the manner of someone carrying credit cards and an iPad. Not that I carry any of those things. (So don't get any ideas, thugs!)

"How you doin'?" he says, spittling. Headphones and downcast eyes don't deter him; he leans right up in my face. "Lemme ask you a favor. Can you give me a dolla?"

"No," I mumble. He is so close that it's impossible to pretend he's not there.

"I write poemsss. You want me to write one for you? Rrright now?" he slurs.

No thanks, Sir Thug. No man has ever written me a poem. I certainly don't want one from a drunken crackhead. And it's just a hunch, but I have a feeling your poem won't be free.

"That's OK," I say, leaning, then stepping a few feet away from him and his fetid breath. Cars fly down High Street. The "Don't Walk" sign shines red.

I'm screwed.

My efforts to move away anger him, I can tell. Fire flashes in his eyes, and he draws closer, looming over me. I pull my purse, which definitely doesn't contain credit cards and an iPad, to my body.

He stares at me for a moment, leers me up and down, then makes a sweeping gesture toward my (admittedly 40-something) stomach.

"You . . . you . . . look like you got a bun in the oven. Ya know what I'm ssssayin'. Heh," he slurs.

This is not a question—it is a mean-spirited declaration. Then, he lurches away, pants-on-the-ground, underwear sagging.

And you had a 12-pack in your stomach by 4 p.m. on a Tuesday, you rude, filthy piece of shit.

I only return his insult silently. Though I have secret bad-ass gangsta skills—and he very much deserves a kick in the 'nads—I don't want even my shoes to touch him. I want him to get the hell away from me. He oozes biohazards.

In my mind, I re-cap:

1. Drunken crackhead thug approached me, violating my personal dance space with his putrefying breath and spit.

2. Drunken crackhead thug asked to write me a poem, for which he wanted me to pay.

3. Drunken crackhead thug insulted my muffin-top belly, and then stumbled away.

The "Walk" sign turns green. Finally. I walk across High Street toward my car, still looking down at the phone and slowly shaking my head.

Growing up and living in a rural area, I used to think that working in the city would be incredible. The freaking *Mary Tyler Moore Show*! I'd walk in the park, trade jokes with Lou Grant, throw my hat in the air.

It's just like that. Except with drunken crackheads. Insulting drunken crackheads. Also there is no Lou Grant, I don't wear hats and I don't want to walk in the park. All I want is to get home. And take off my bra.

CHAPTER FORTY-ONE
The Left Lane Is the New Right Lane. Apparently
Thursday, 6:18 p.m.

Five thousand people on the interstate this evening.

Not one of them can drive.

Except for me, of course. I'm a fantastic driver—according to me.

And lest you doubt my freeway tally during rush hour, let me assure you: It's true. I know because I counted cars. I have time to do so because I'm stuck, always stuck, behind Rusty McLeftLane.

Hey, did you know? The left lane is the new right lane. Apparently.

What's that, you say? The passing lane is for, of all things, passing? Hahaha—surely you jest; I'm afraid you've got it all wrong. Each and every day, I manage to become first in line behind Rusty, who cruises 50 mph in the left lane, mile after oblivious mile, as if it's a country road on a Sunday afternoon. Trapped behind him are 49 cars, 49 homicidal drivers and 49 pairs of headlights—angrily glaring headlights.

I can see them in the rearview mirror, burning with the livid heat of a thousand suns. And judging by the bobbing lights, my fellow motorists are growing increasingly hostile and impatient, riding my tail, swerving around, flashing high-beams. It's always at this point of the day where I decide again that something about the highway turns nice, stable, tax-paying people into Satan's spawn.

Yep. Instant asshole: Just add freeway.

Recent research states that people with commutes of more than 30 miles die younger than those who live closer to their workplace. I believe it. Because it doesn't matter who it is: neighbors, church-goers, sweet little old ladies—we all become mortal enemies on the road, plotting revenge, flashing hand gestures, brandishing concealed weapons . . .

During my commute, I once narrowly missed a collision with a driver who had pulled out six feet in front of me. He proceeded to drive 20 mph in a 55 mph zone, so I passed his battered, muddy pickup, and this angered him so badly that he raced his vehicle back around mine, then yanked a large knife from under his seat. He waved the thing at me in the rear windshield, and then stabbed it into his dashboard.

I think of this fine fellow today as I endure the angry mob currently crawling up my rear, the one that collected as a result of McLeftLane in front of me. They're getting ready to blow; it will be any minute now. Five, four, three, two . . . and here he comes: Asshole Number One.

Yeah, I see you over there, sneaking up, stealing along my passenger side, because, hey, the right lane is the new left lane—according to you. So you think I'm going too slow; think I'm going to let you squeeze in, don't you?

Dream on, pal. Relax and enjoy that right lane. You're not going anywhere.

You thought I was holding you back, didn't you, Number One? Now that you're up here, you can see that we're all at the mercy of Rusty McLeftLane. He's lost in the 50s on a country road. We mustn't interrupt his reverie.

Driving. Everyone else is doing it wrong, and Number One and the rest of the assholes follow a set of rules entirely of their own. Not for them, those silly roadway regulations, and based on many years of observation, I have been able to decipher Asshole Code as it relates to standard traffic laws:

Obey all speed limits.

Asshole Code: Unless you're in the left lane. Or the right lane.

Bah. Screw the speed limit.

Don't tailgate or follow too closely.

Asshole Code: Unless you're late or in a hurry. In that case, ride some ass like a frat boy on a Saturday night.

Don't use your cell phone while driving.

Asshole Code: Unless you need to make a call . . . or send a text . . . or check Facebook.

Always use your rearview mirrors.

Asshole Code: For checking your hair, doing your makeup and glaring at people.

Be a courteous driver.

Asshole Code: Unless you're in a bad mood. In that case, feel free to brandish a weapon.

Ah . . . it's pleasant, daydreaming like this, pondering the laws that others ignore.

But the angry bright lights in my mirror tell me it's time to snap back to reality. I need to focus my helpful guidance again on Mr. McLeftLane.

Dear Rusty: It's great that you're not in a hurry. How nice for you! Did you know that it's 5:35 p.m., Thursday evening on I-70? Did you know that the minimum legal speed of an Interstate is 45 mph? Did you know your turn signal's blinked for the last 27 miles?

If you'd look up, you'd see that the 49 sets of headlights behind you are in a bit of a, well, a pickle. Personally, I've been away from home for most of the day; I've got kids to boss around, a husband to nag, a glass of wine I'd really like to pour—Very Important Stuff.

Sometimes, Rusty, I can't help but think it would be nice to live in your world. Never rush-rush-rushing to make it to the next appointment, the next event, just to get up tomorrow and do it all again.

Maybe you've got something there. Maybe I should do it: Don a jaunty cap, hop in a Buick, tie up the passing lane.

But right now, I've got Number One swerving beside me, and the rest of the assholes riding my rear.

And if they don't kill me, you, Rusty McLeftLane, you might let me get home. By, say, Sunday?

CHAPTER FORTY-TWO
I Sleep with a Jackhammer, a Chainsaw and a Grizzly Bear
Tuesday, 1:51 a.m.

Breathing: He's doing it wrong. He could definitely use my guidance.

"Hey!" I elbow him. "Roll over! You're snoring too loud!"

"Mmmfff?" he mumbles.

"I said you're snoring loud again! *Roll over!*"

"OK, OK," he sighs and turns on his side. "*Zzzz-shooooo . . .*"

Jay-sus. No wonder I haven't slept through the night since I was single.

1:51 a.m. Welcome to our bed, folks, where the average nightly decibel level rivals that of the Daytona 500. Take a middle-aged male with undiagnosed sleep apnea. Add a middle-aged female with a hormonal brain full of needless worry and anger.

What do you get?

One cheerfully oblivious sleeping man—and one bitchy woman who has considered the creative possibilities of duct tape.

The only way I can block the noise is by sandwiching my head between two king-size pillows; so I grab them, as I do every night, and try to go back to sleep.

I try.

"*Zzzzz-shooooooo . . .*"

Lord, that man is loud. He says I snore. This is patently false, and even if it were true, I am sure I would do so in a soft, ladylike manner, like a lovely deer asleep in the meadow.

He, on the other hand, sounds like a sick rhinoceros. He sounds like a wounded moose. He sounds like 80 mph hurricane winds, mixed with an approaching tsunami; like a tornado, combined with a jackhammer combined with, somehow, a very angry bear.

131

"*Zzzzz-shooooo . . .*"

Pillows still smashed over each ear, I scoot as far away from him as possible, until I teeter precariously on the very edge of the mattress. Thanks, Sir Snores-A-Lot, I'm wide awake now, my eyes open, my mind racing with hormones and worries and memories and to-do lists and, thrown in for shits and giggles, a Maroon 5 song on an endless loop.

"*You and I go hard . . .*"

Mmmm. Adam Levine. I'm sure he *could* go hard. Not a bad thought to have at 2:19 a.m. Tall, fit, sexy eyes—certain parts of my body start to tingle. I think I'll just lay here and think of young Mr. Levine for a while, picture him under twisted sheets, the things he could do with all that tantric yoga experience, the positions he could . . .

"**Snort-snort* Zzzz-shooooo . . .*"

Yeah. Goodbye, Adam Levine.

Ugh. 3 a.m. now, eyes wide open. Might as well pull up Google here on the phone and do some research. What I find is most interesting:

Fact: An estimated fifty percent of Americans snore. Loudly.

Fact: From the sound of things, they're all here, in bed, beside me.

Fact: Snoring can cause hearing loss in the snorer's spouse.

Fact: I can't hear for shit.

Fact: Partners of snorers report high levels of fatigue, sleepiness and night-time Googling.

Fact: I found this out by Googling, "my husband snores like a chainsaw."

"*Zzzzzz-shooooo . . .*"

3:36 a.m. I close out of Google, and roll on my back. His snoring is proof that he can annoy me even in his sleep. My fatigued, sleep-deprived brain begins to fantasize, about hurting him. Just a little, you understand, just enough to stop the chainsaw. I have already, over the years, elbowed, kicked, and slapped him. One of these days, he'll get a cock-punch.

It's really just a matter of time.

"*Zzzz-shooooo . . .*"

3:56 a.m. I grab the pillows, sit up in bed and start to ease my way off. Less than an hour to go until I have to get up and shower for work; I need some rest. I'm going to the couch. He hates when I leave. No matter how quietly I roll out, he hears me, and we have the same conversation.

"Where you goin'?" he mumbles.

"I'm sleeping on the couch. You're snoring. Loud."

He sighs. "We'll probably end up one of those couples, won't we? The ones who have separate bedrooms."

"Sounds like a great idea. I'll draw up the plans," I mumble, heading for the door.

"*Zzzz-shooooo . . .*"

Yeah. I can tell he's very concerned.

I shuffle to the living room, flop down and nestle into the sofa, hoping for peace and the last 50 minutes of shut-eye and maybe a little more Adam Levine.

Huddled there, I think about the early years, when love was new, the breathing young, soft and quiet, and we slept close together, cuddled side by side. I'd have never pictured us inches away, let alone rooms apart, from each other.

As I finally drift off, I pray that it doesn't come down to two different bedrooms. In my overnight Googling, I've read that couples who deal with snoring and sleep apnea have a very high divorce rate, mostly stemming from the fact that they end up sleeping separately.

Although his noise causes me to sometimes fantasize about duct tape and the odd cock-punch, I do adore that guy. Sometimes, on the rare occasions that I don't hear him snoring, I even check to make sure he's breathing. I'm loving like that.

Anyway, we have already been married 20 years. Might as well stick it out.

But I'll tell you one thing:

I am really fucking tired.

CHAPTER FORTY-THREE
Crack Whore Dawn, What's That Flower You Have On?
Wednesday, 8:30 p.m.

I go to bed every night as Dawn.

But I wake up each morning as Crack Whore Dawn.

My friends try to comfort me. They tell me this is normal, just another sign of middle age, that I arise each day looking like a crack whore version of myself, worse yet, the crack-whore *older* version of myself.

Every morning, when I stumble into the bathroom and glance into the mirror, the near-stranger staring back at me resembles a battered old hooker/crackhead. Greasy, sweaty hair sticking sideways, smeared leftover makeup, eyes puffed almost closed, deep sleep creases on the cheeks and chest, and wouldn't you know it, a few zits thrown in.

Ah, middle age. Wrinkles *and* acne—a double delight!

My disheveled appearance stems from the fact that I spend all night rolling around, wide awake, sweating, and not for any kind of exciting reason related to sex, crack or rock 'n roll. No, I simply cannot sleep.

Thanks to my spouse's incessant snoring, and the fact that I'm possibly perimenopausal, sleep just keeps growing ever more difficult for me. My brain does not switch off. It reels in circles, hashing and re-hashing a never-ending list of thoughts, concerns and worries.

Back in the early 90s, I also rolled around, sweating and losing lots of sleep, but that was for fun-zies. These days, I have only one goal in the bedroom, and it's shuteye. Ask my husband. He'll tell you.

Just like tonight, as I sink into bed. It's way late, 8:30 p.m. and all, so I throw myself onto the mattress for another relaxing night of *not* sleeping.

I toss. I turn. I sweat.

Then, I feel someone staring at me. Longingly, lovingly, disturbingly staring at me.

I open my eyes. "What?"

He smiles. Oh, great. I can tell. The husband wants to touch my swimsuit areas.

"No way," I say. "We just did that last week. I'm tired. It's, like, 8:30 and stuff."

More smile.

"Seriously. You know we have to get up at five. Not tonight."

"I'm just looking at you," he says.

Yeah. He's looking at me alright, with a grin. A grin that says, "Lose the yoga pants." A grin that caused two children.

"Give me four minutes," he says. "Three if you wiggle around a little."

I can tell there is no getting out of this.

"OK," I tell him. "But make it snappy. I'm beat."

He is true to his efficient promise, and soon enough, I locate my crumbled yoga pants at the foot of the bed, pull them back on and flop gratefully back to my pillow.

The romance. It's palpable.

None of this is his fault; since I've hit my mid-forties, I have the sex drive of a chair.

Also, nookie is yet another item on a very long list of things that keep me awake. So here I lie, in the dark, eyes wide open.

I toss. I turn. I sweat.

One hour and forty-seven frustrating minutes later, I roll over and fumble around in the top drawer of the nightstand, where I have a miniature pharmacy of products to help me sleep, including—but not limited to—melatonin, ear plugs, an eye mask, Vick's Vapor Rub to dab under my nose, and several bottles of sleep aids. I fish around for my current favorite, Benadryl, but I can't find it. I flip on the light and rummage around in the drawer below it.

This second drawer, my sad little Walmart Fountain of Youth, won't even shut. It is stuffed with an entire arsenal of products to beat back time and Crack Whore Dawn.

There's your standard lotions, SPF lotions, day lotions and night lotions. There's your alpha-hydroxies, your soothing gels, your pore-reducers, your exfoliators, your tone-enhancers and your anti-oxidants; not to mention the retinol gel that I may or may not have purchased from an illegal online Canadian pharmacy.

And don't get me started on the eye creams. They have their own drawer.

Unable to find the Benadryl, I pop a melatonin, shut the nightstand and hope for the best.

I toss. I turn. I sweat. And before I know it . . .

Beep-beep-beep-beep!

It's 5 a.m. I don't need this alarm, of course; I'm wide awake, and I have been all night long. I hoist myself out of bed and stumble into the bathroom.

And there she is again: Crack Whore Dawn. The strongest thing she got into last night was the melatonin, but once again, she resembles her own mug shot after a really rough night on the town. The derelict in the mirror also looks like someone beat the hell out of her, like someone hit her upside the face, chest and head with a major appliance or something.

It looks like she's gone 15 rounds with George Foreman. And his grill.

"Good morning, beautiful," the husband mumbles, stumbling into the bathroom. Yeah. His eyes are starting to go.

I peel off my clothes and step into the shower, taking note of the many other ways time and gravity have pummeled me, the chins, breasts and belly that fall farther south each day. They're all signs of my impending demise, my foot in the grave.

I smile a crazy crack-whore smile, because I am most certainly lurching toward decrepitude. But you know what? So is everyone else.

And waking up—even as an apparent crack whore—beats the hell out of *not* waking up.

CHAPTER FORTY-FOUR
The Monkeys in My Mind Need Bitch-Slapped
Friday, 4:21 a.m.

There's no cure for it.

There's no prescription, no diagnosis, no loud, embarrassing telethon. There's absolutely nothing you can do.

It just stays there, hiding in the background; lurking, festering, annoying, then popping back up to cause misery—like a cold sore, a computer virus, a Rush Limbaugh.

I get it every single day—several hundred times.

What is it, you ask?

A case of The Shoulds.

It begins every morning, when my eyes, in direct opposition to all good reasoning and the rest of my body, pop open at 4:21 a.m.

I should get up.

This is a lie. I really don't *have* to get up until 5 a.m., but The Shoulds, they say, you guessed it, that I should.

I remain in bed, but my perimenopausal monkey-mind jumps from tree to metaphorical tree, swinging from branches of Shoulds:

I should change these sheets.

I should clean this bedroom.

I should be a better housekeeper/wife/mother/daughter.

I should be a better person.

The clock now reads 4:22.

Four-plus Shoulds.

One minute.

Sigh

I should get a shower.

This? I can manage. So I roll out of bed and into the bathroom, stripping off my PJs. Then, I look in the mirror.

Big mistake:

I should lose weight.

I should stick to my diet.

I should lift weights more often.

I should increase my cardio.

I should do some yoga.

4:26 a.m. Five minutes of consciousness, several dozen Shoulds.

I really should get in the shower.

I manage to keep the should-monkeys at bay long enough to bathe and dress, but they return in force as I walk into Should Central, a.k.a. the kitchen.

I should clean these counters.

I should sweep this floor.

I should give that dog a bath.

I should thaw something for dinner.

I should make those kids eat more vegetables.

I work on some Shoulds, and corral all the monkeys I can before leaving for work. I pack lunches, wipe down counters and fill out school paperwork; I load the dishwasher and water the dog and thaw something for dinner. I slide my cell phone into my purse, and grab the car keys.

5:17 a.m. Time to wake him.

"Hey," I say, walking into the bedroom. "You should get up now."

"Mmfffttt?"

The husband does not know the S-word of which I speak. Empty, is his mind, of worries, of concern, of monkeys.

Empty, is his mind, of Shoulds.

He does everything he *must* do, but not, in my valuable opinion, everything he *should* do. No, he just goes about his day smiling, laughing, chilling out, then snoring and sleeping.

All of this is very annoying.

"I *said* you should get up now. It's almost 5:20."

"I don't have to get up till 5:30," he mumbles.

"Well," I say, "you really should get up now so you don't have to rush into work. Also, if you leave soon, there'll be a lot less assholes on the road."

"*Zzzz-shooooo . . .*"

Yeah. I'll have what he's having. He doesn't seem concerned about his harried commute.

I am, so I grab my stuff and head to the car.

I-should-wash-this-thing-I-should-vacuum-the-interior-I-should-get-the-oil-changed.

But I should have done all that last weekend. So I clip on my employee

ID, coast down the driveway and simultaneously pull up the Pandora app. I turn right onto I-70, mash down the accelerator, and join the fray.

I should drive slower.

True, however . . .

I should get to work on time.

When did it happen? When did *I should*—and its evil cousins *I need* and *I better*—become such rules, such commands, such mantras of mine?

When did should become such a verb?

I know what you're saying: "Should *always* has been a verb. An auxiliary verb, to be exact."

You're also saying, "You're crazy."

Well—you may be right. I may be crazy.

Speaking of old songs and Billy Joel, there was a time, two or three decades ago, when monkeys didn't prance on my back, and Shoulds didn't matter.

They seem like Polaroid snapshots, these memories. They were nothing life-changing, just little slices of days, small moments of pure happiness: lying in the sun, riding a bike no-hands, laughing with friends around a fire.

I remember, back then, looking forward to things. I remember fun and joy and living in the moment.

Most of all, I remember when life wasn't one big to-do list.

That's a nice story, Grandma. But you should focus on the now.

Now. It's 2013. Already.

Really, I have no reason to worry. I have two healthy kids, a good job, a nice home, and a wonderful—if decidedly Should-free—husband.

5:54 a.m.

I should maybe get a grip.

I should possibly see a shrink.

I should probably . . .

just . . .

relax.

CHAPTER FORTY-FIVE
Decaf Coffee: Why Bother?
Tuesday, 5:58 a.m.

In an effort to be less of a bitch, I have given up caffeine.

Please. Hold me. There goes my energy, my creativity, my ambition, my intelligence and my sanity.

You see, along with smartphones, dishwashers and a nice glass of merlot, I believe that caffeine is proof that God loves us. It helps with all of life's unpleasant activities, such as waking up, standing and speaking to people before 10 a.m. It gets me out of bed and to the kitchen before I can consider my options.

I've long used caffeine, in the form of coffee, to complete other objectionable tasks, such as going to work. I've spent most of my career in marketing, and every day, every minute of my job is a struggle to stay awake, awash, as I am, in numbers and statistics and typical corporate silliness.

Worse, I recently received a "promotion" (read: same pay/more work), and now I *write* about numbers, statistics and other BS. I am supposed to produce interesting articles, using terms like "scalable," "depreciation" and "productize."

I'm not even sure what "scalable," "depreciation" and "productize" mean. They have certainly overestimated my "skill set."

Wading through words like these requires coffee. There are times it has been solely responsible for keeping me awake in my cubicle.

It helps at home, too. Behind every functioning mother is a pot of strong coffee. And I wish my family would figure this out after all these years, because they seem to have mistaken me for someone who wants to talk at 7 b.c. (before coffee):

Husband: "Where are my car keys?"

Me: "I don't know."

Princess: "Mom—where are my cheer shoes?"

Me: "I don't know."

Hobo: "'Mornin', Mommy. How are you doing?"

Me: "I don't *know*!"

Yeah. Things are bad when you start yelling at the baby.

I have a problem; just ask them. Too little coffee, and I can't function. Too much, and I become a wild-eyed, shouting banshee, scattering the husband and children to three corners of the house where they hunker down—frightened, shivering, alone.

Can't live with it and can't live without it. Caffeine is my crack cocaine. Life has become a war between Decaf Dawn and Full-Caff Dawn.

Full-Caff Dawn is a feisty go-getter with a gleam in her eye, a spring in her step, four cups down her gullet. Need a floor scrubbed? A basement dug? A 2,000-word article on "depreciation"? Full-Caff Dawn's your gal.

Unfortunately, Full-Caff Dawn can be hell on heels, filled with impatience and misplaced aggression and downright evil. Full-Caff Dawn hates traffic. Full-Caff Dawn hates crowds of people.

Full-Caff Dawn hates everyone.

Decaf Dawn, on the other hand, is a gentler soul. She's a slower mover; a drooler of spittle, a shuffler of feet, with the carriage and demeanor of a hung-over bum.

Need a slacker? A loafer? A taker of naps? Decaf Dawn's got all this— and much, much less. Thanks to her addled thoughts and general malaise, she is too confused to be angry, too tired to think.

Just this morning, feeling very tragic, I slouched to the kitchen for a cup of decaffeinated coffee.

How do I take my decaf? Quickly. And don't be handing me any weak, old-lady, Sanka shit. That's like drinking water—water with an aftertaste. I like my coffee like I like my men: strong, hot and ready to serve me in the morning.

Now, it used to be I had two answers when the question was decaf, these were "No!" and "Hell, no!" Decaffeinated coffee was, to me, like non-alcoholic beer. Why bother?

But coffee producers have come a long way since Sanka. Starbucks makes a decent off-the-shelf decaf now. It tastes OK, and though I don't consider it real coffee, the placebo effect helps Decaf Dawn function.

This morning, while I wait for it to brew, I decide to do some research into my obvious addiction, so I Google "Coffee is my crack."

I find many interesting things, which are all on the Internet, and therefore completely, 100 percent factual:

In its pure state, caffeine is a crystalline white powder.

What did I tell you? Crack cocaine.

More than 450,000,000 cups of coffee are consumed every day.

The rest of the people get their caffeine from tea, and they're mostly British, so no one cares.

Caffeine can increase feelings of well-being. It does this by raising levels of dopamine.

A.k.a. dope, a.k.a. again—what did I tell you? Crack cocaine. Better living through chemistry, that's what I always say.

But caffeine isn't all sunshine and roses and drug addiction. It has its issues:

Withdrawal can cause headache, fatigue, anxiety, difficulty concentrating . . .

. . . bad decisions, mismatched socks, Ozzy Osbourne . . .

Caffeine consumed in the afternoon can cause insomnia.

And I haven't slept through the night since, well, ever.

Caffeine is the most popular drug in the world. Ninety percent of North Americans drink it on a daily basis.

The other 10 percent? Are asleep.

All the data certainly supports my coffee/crack theory, and as I finish reading the statistics, my lame-o pot of decaf Starbucks spurts to a stop. The noise wakes the husband, who walks into the kitchen yawning and scratching and once again mistaking me for someone who wants to talk.

And hug.

"Good morning, honey," he says, reaching for me.

"What?!"

"Wow. You really don't seem to be much cheerier," he says, crossing his arms and smirking. "How's that decaf thing working out for ya?"

I fill my mug, turn around and shuffle out the door for work.

"I don't know!"

CHAPTER FORTY-SIX
Come Here, Vodka. You Look Like a Bad Decision
Sunday, 8:29 p.m.

Ah, the countryside—where septic tanks are only an option.

That's what I thought and "Oh shit!" is what I said, as I tumbled into the brown, murky depths of a local lake famous for the fact that several toilets in surrounding homes and businesses flush directly into it.

Lost my smartphone in the crappy lake that night. Lost several other things with it—my music, my photos, my social networks, my sanity. Lost my very soul.

What happened, you ask?

Vodka. Vodka happened.

Normally, I am a reasonable person, a social drinker, content, on a Friday night, with a beer or three. Give me almost any cheap American brew in a can: your Coors Light, your Miller Lite, your Bud Light—even a PBR will do.

Klassy with a K, that's me.

But last Friday, things were different. We had gone boating with friends, which doesn't happen often, and so I was feeling kind of devil-may-care, kind of celebratory. I was feeling kind of . . .

Vodka.

No, I don't drink it often, and when the boater's girlfriend offered to mix me up a vodka-filled Purple Hooter, well, it seemed like a good idea at the time.

"Sure! That sounds great!"

There are reasons that I usually just drink bad beer. I drink it because it tastes like: A) Sweat; B) Water; or C) Sweaty water.

When a beverage tastes like A, B or C, I tend to drink it a bit slower, because it sucks. And when a drink tastes good, when it tastes like a sugary tropical treat, well, I suck it down like it's a sugary tropical treat.

And then I ask for another one.

So it went that I was a couple of Purple Hooters in the bag, riding across the lake with the husband and our boater friends. We motored around for several hours, marveling at the gorgeous homes, the stars, the cool, dark evening, and though we were having a blast, I didn't feel tipsy at all—just relaxed and happy.

But relaxed and happy is not my natural state. No, I do not know this thing you call "relaxed and happy," and something had to come along to knock me off balance.

Enter vodka.

The end of the evening arrived, and we parked the boat in front of a restaurant close to the location of our car. We sat for a bit, talking and laughing, the ladies slurping the last of our Purple Hooters. After a while, I looked at the time.

"Whoa," I said. "It's 11:45. My eyes will pop open at 4:30. We have to go."

I stood up—without incident, I might add—and gathered my things: a sweatshirt, a ball cap and a little wallet with a carabineer clip that held my driver's license and phone—safely. I attached this wallet around my belt loop—safely. I prepared to exit the boat—safely.

I have a theory that different types of alcohol affect people in different ways. Wine makes some weepy, beer can make folks surly and tequila makes you pregnant.

And vodka? Vodka makes me clumsy, apparently, because that's when it happened.

Vodka happened.

As I stepped off the boat safely, with my cell phone clipped to me safely, my foot, in a willful, unsafe manner, underestimated the location of the dock.

And Dawn fell in the soup with her smartphone.

I sank right to the bottom and kicked my way off the questionable muck, losing in the process my pride, my flip-flops and have I mentioned my phone? Oh, my phone.

My precious.

I broke the surface and flailed around like a drowning lunatic. The dock lay several feet above my soaking wet head; there was no ladder to climb out of the lake. My husband and fellow boaters came over and hauled me up—after they finished doubling over in laughter.

My phone. She slept with the fishes. As I wrung out my clothes, I searched the "water" (a.k.a. sewage), but I couldn't see her in the dark brown soup. I wasn't going back in there, though. Oh *hell* no.

And that's how my no-good, very bad weekend without a smartphone began. I felt idiotic and lost because, like most folks, I use my phone for almost everything these days: work, writing, music, photos, entertainment, and constant contact with people via texting and social networks like Facebook. Oh, Facebook. My precious.

Saturday morning, I moaned and paced dejectedly around the house until the Verizon store opened, and then I raced to town to begin the process of replacing the drowned smartphone.

I had one stroke of luck in the whole soggy mess: I'd purchased insurance on the device. Insurance, I might add, that I'd nearly canceled the week before because Verizon had raised the price. I'd carried the letter they sent about the rate increase in my purse for two weeks, meaning to cancel the policy, but luckily, I never quite got around to it. Sometimes, not having one's shit together pays off.

At the store and in a frenzy, I filled out the paperwork necessary to get another device. The new phone would normally be delivered the next day, but of course, it was Saturday, of course it was, and my smartphone wouldn't arrive until Monday. Of course it wouldn't.

I drove home, where I spent the entire weekend without my phone, my lifeline, my precious. The husband loaned me his crappy no-contract phone, his "Obama-phone" as I call it, for outings, but still, I felt despondent. I had no instant access to Pandora or Spotify, so I was forced to listen to commercial, and by that I mean lots of fucking commercials, radio.

Oh, the humanity.

Also, as I mentioned, I now had no quick access to social networks, to Facebook, Twitter or Pinterest. I had to have actual, non-virtual interactions with actual, real people. It just about killed me.

All in all, it was a very long, very miserable weekend without my smartphone until I replaced it with this one, a weekend full of commercials, real verbal conversations and, worst of all, nothing to do on the toilet.

You might call these first-world problems. I call them misery.

Then again, you know what they say: If you stumble, make it part of the dance; and if you fall into a shitty lake, make it part of your book. Yes, at least I got a story out of this. And hepatitis—probably hepatitis. But what can I say? Vodka happens.

CHAPTER FORTY-SEVEN
Got a Man? Get Some Bleach
Saturday, 8:30 p.m.

He walks out of the bedroom, sniffing his fingers. Then he washes his hands—voluntarily.

I am afraid to ask.

"Don't ask," he says. "You don't want to know."

We've been married a long time. I already know. He has just been scratching a southern region.

He is *always* scratching a southern region.

I am pleased that he washed his hands without coercion, though. This is new for him, exciting for me, as I have just cleaned and wiped down the kitchen—with bleach.

I am *always* wiping things down—with bleach.

Next, I pull a fresh, clean dish towel from the cupboard and hang it up. And as I stand here, drinking coffee and admiring my spotless, sanitized counter, I watch him turn from the sink, lift the dish towel, wipe his runny nose with it, and put it back.

Apparently, where I see a dish towel, he sees a Kleenex.

"Why don't you just wipe your ass with that, too?" I ask.

I see this as sarcasm. He sees it as a dare.

Suffice it to say the dish towel goes immediately into the washer—with bleach.

Men: the very reason for bleach. So many of them seem to have a need to scratch, wipe and spew bodily fluids everywhere, blessing all they survey with their liquids, gases and bacteria. You see it on the schoolyard: little boys spitting on the ground. You see it in the back yard: men peeing outside.

You damn-sure see it in a hotel room, with any decent black-light.

Honestly, I don't know why I try to change what has been firmly ingrained in his biology, but I do, and for 20 years now, I've been engaged in a fervent and altogether futile education process with my husband regarding basic hygiene. First lesson: *Hey! You! Get Out of My Towel!*

You heard me. My ass: good. His ass: bad.

Individual bath towels are to be used by one person and one person alone. That way, each user protects his/her own ass/face area. I use one side of the towel for my face and upper body, and the other side for my lovely lady bits, and never the twain shall meet.

That is, simply put, how you maintain cootie control.

But not everyone believes this. Let me set the scene for you. The repeating, ongoing, never-ending scene:

4:35 a.m. The husband has just finished his shower, and where I have hung up my fresh, clean, barely used bath towel the day before, he sees his fresh, clean, barely used bath towel.

"How considerate of her," he thinks, *"to pull out a new towel out for me! Again!"*

He proceeds to dry his face, body and all manner of hairy personal regions with what was once my towel.

My clean, lovely lady-towel.

But I don't know this yet, so fast forward to 5:05 a.m. as I step out of the shower—shivering, barely awake and sopping wet. Water pours down from my hair, stinging and blinding me. Eyes squeezed shut, I pray that this time, it'll be OK. This time, he's changed his ways. This time, I'll grab a dry towel, the clean one I put out the day before.

Still blind, still groping, I reach out for the peg. I extend my arm, stand on my tiptoes, stretch my fingers . . . and I find it. Cold. Soaking wet. Used. Once more, he's taken my clean, lovely lady-towel, and used it to dry his wet, hairy man-body. I am forced to immediately throw the used towel in the laundry—with bleach.

Then I get out a new towel, which he uses; so I get out another new towel, he uses that one. Repeat this scene every morning for 20 years, and you can imagine my frustration—and homicidal tendencies.

Oh, I've tried. I've begged. I've pleaded.

I've cried.

From time to time, I march out of the bathroom completely nude, holding sopping terry-cloth, and present the *Get Out of My Towel!* education program.

I wave it at him. I say, "Do you want to dry your face where I dried my ass?" I explain: "This is your face. This is my ass. I dried my ass on this towel. Do you want to rub it on your face?" I point out the different areas, "Ass . . . face . . . ass . . . face" until eventually, I become nauseated . . .

. . . and he becomes aroused.

Blood drains from his head into regions further south and the hygiene lesson becomes a big FAIL, because my nakedness and gestures have plainly indicated that I'm ready for a session of groping and dry-humping.

What's the best time for fondling? Anytime. What's the best place? Anywhere. I pass by him? Great time to grab my ass. I'm lying beside him? Fab time to grope my boob.

And if I bend over in his vicinity, my stooped posture plainly indicates that I want him and I should be vigorously faux-humped. Doesn't matter where he is, what I'm doing, like a nine-month-old puppy, he runs up behind me, usually fully clothed, and pumps away.

"*She's tying her shoes?*" is the thought process. "*Perhaps I should hump her!*"

"*She's reaching for a skillet,*" he thinks. "*How convenient of her to bend over so I can hump her!*"

"*She's lifting a laundry basket?*" he ponders. "*She's overwhelmed with sexual desire and I should mount her at once!*"

I have a theory about all this. Of course I do. It is not based on any science or research, because, really: scientific facts? You're reading the wrong book.

But, after many decades of closely observing my husband, I've decided that these habits, the spitting, the scratching, the spewing and humping, stem from caveman roots, instincts necessary to ensure survival of the species.

Way back when, cavemen protected and expanded their families by marking territory, and they did this the way all animals do: by peeing on, spitting at and mounting nearly everything—all the time.

So thanks to their caveman heritage, many males just see things differently than females; they see certain actions and bodily functions as a fence—a signal, if you will—for other males to stay away.

But I am a woman, and I'll tell you what I see: germs, biohazards and gratuitous humping.

And all these nasty habits do is make me want to take a shower, with bleach, which I'm sure will be fine with my caveman. He's about due for a new towel anyway. A clean, lovely lady towel.

CHAPTER FORTY-EIGHT
I Miss Grandma. I Don't Miss Her Haircuts
Monday, 7:14 a.m.

My hair: a complete disappointment since 1969.

Yeah, that's the year I was born. What about it? I came into this world with unfortunate hair. I'll leave this world with unfortunate hair—if there's any left at all.

My hair is colorless, lifeless and downright thin. Hairdressers call it "fine" to ease the sting. But there's no getting around it. You can call it "fine," but it's "thin" to the point that I'll eventually be "bald."

I've tried to change it. My grandmother—she tried to change it. Futile yet frugal attempts to improve my 'do date back to the Nixon administration.

"Fifteen dollars for a haircut? Ha! No way. Bring me the Scotch tape and scissors."

Oh, Lordie. Scotch tape, the scissors and my grandmother: never a successful combination.

But there was no telling her that. She was a child of the Great Depression, and paying someone else to do something she could accomplish ranked as a totally foreign concept. Anyway, It was 1974. We did as we were told.

I'd been through this many times before, and there was no use arguing. I handed her the Scotch tape and scissors, then assumed my perch on the folding stool for the inevitable.

"Let me just get it in a straight line here . . . "

I squirmed as she taped the width of my forehead, tickling me and smashing hair down into my eyes. She squinted through bifocals—her bad vision was a running family joke—and I watched as the sharp scissors rose to my terrified eyeballs.

"Hold still now!"

I squeezed my eyes shut and held my breath.

Scritch-scritch-scritch

She cut across my bangs, then ripped off the tape, my hair, and several dozen eyelashes.

"Ow-uhhh!"

"There!" she said. "Much better. Fifteen dollars for a salon haircut? Ha! Look at this!"

She gave me a mirror. Gone were my bangs. Gone was my dignity.

Gone were half my eyebrows.

The length of my hair, thin, raggedy, dishwater blonde, fell limply onto my shoulders. She hadn't touched that. But my bangs, cut in a razor-straight, Scotch-taped line, rose high on my forehead. I looked like an orphan. I looked like a little beggar.

I looked like I qualified for state assistance.

Things didn't improve much in the 80s, especially on the day I saw Grandma frowning thoughtfully at me from the kitchen.

"Bring me that box of Toni perm in the closet. And get a big bath towel."

Oh, Lordie. There went my plan of roller-disco in the garage all day. The Toni Home Perm, the bath towel, my grandmother—once more, never a successful combination.

But again, there was no telling her that, and I don't know if I've mentioned it, but we did as we were told.

I climbed up on the stool. I was older, of course, bigger in 1981, but still topped with unfortunate hair. I sorted the rollers, white and pink, as she opened the bottles. Toxic fumes wafted into the kitchen, and I settled onto the stool for my chemical fate.

"OK. Hand me a pink one, and a wrapping paper."

She didn't have to tell me. I'd been through this countless times. I knew the drill: minutes, days, months, it seemed, of pink and white rollers; hours, years, millenniums of combing, yanking and pulling.

"Ow-uhhh!"

"Oh, hush," she said. "And sit still! You'll be here a while. We have got to do something with this mop!"

As you can tell, Grandma was a mild-mannered, soft-spoken woman.

But my straight hair infuriated her; it was an affront. She came from an entire generation of wavy-haired women; the way she saw it, all female hair was required, by federal law, to be curled. The fact that my "mop" simply wouldn't hold any sort of style was completely unacceptable. That's where the Toni perm and half an afternoon came in.

Four hours of yanking. Four hours of dizzying fumes. Four hours of my life that I'll never get back later, she handed me the mirror.

"There!" she said. "Thirty dollars for a salon perm? Ha! No way. Look at that!"

Oh, I saw it alright. My shoulder-length, stick-straight strands had, thanks to the sweat, expertise and hard work of my grandmother, shriveled up and died. There was no curl.

There was barely any hair.

My coif's only redeeming quality, its decent length, was gone. What was left of it was frizz. And more frizz. From the back, my head looked like Ronald McDonald's. If Ronald McDonald was a 12-year-old dishwater blonde on public assistance.

That was about the last time I remember climbing onto Grandma's stool. Soon enough, I became a teenager and began actually caring about what I looked like. It was time to begin the futile process of attempting to style my hair all by myself. I fried and flipped it for the Farrah, I whacked and hacked it for the she-mullet.

But those Scotch-taped, toxic memories from my grandmother's kitchen remain vivid, unforgettable, and completely terrifying. I can only laugh and shake my limp locks in disbelief now, because it's decades later, and she is long gone.

Not everything has changed though; I still have unfortunate hair. Nowadays, I choose to violate it with hair color, attempting to mix the blonde, the brown and gray into one uniform-looking color, one that doesn't scream "dishwater" and "public assistance."

I color it myself—you're damn right I do—every six weeks with a box of Preference by L'Oreal, purchased from Walmart or Kroger for about $9.

I'm totally worth it.

Anyway, I am *not* going to a stylist for that. Ninety dollars for salon hair color? Ha! No way.

I still think of my grandmother each morning when I look in the mirror, as I yank and pull and try in vain to get my mop to do something besides hang at the shoulders. And I can almost see her in the mirror, behind my reflection.

Frowning thoughtfully.

CHAPTER FORTY-NINE
Fuck You, Running. You Too, Scale
Wednesday, 6:49 a.m.

I was in a really great mood.

And then I weighed myself.

Disgusted, I stepped off the scale one afternoon about three months ago and realized that I had been dieting since the days of big hair and Blondie. I'd been dieting since I was 14.

I'd been dieting since puberty.

In those 30 years, I had tried it all: the cabbage soup diet, the grapefruit diet, the liquid diet, the vegetarian diet, the Atkins diet, the South Beach diet, the drive-an-hour-to-the-doctor-who-prescribes-questionable-diet-pills-diet.

I had tried aerobics, weight training, walking, spinning, swimming, yoga, Pilates, Yogilates, and, for the last two years, I'd tried running.

It's true. On a fateful afternoon three months ago, a day when I stepped on the scale and weighed the most I'd ever weighed and my pants were the tightest they'd ever been, I'd been running for exercise five days a week.

Running. Down the street. With *no one* chasing me.

What did I get for all this running? Well, judging by the scale, I received 11 extra pounds. I also obtained a sore back, sore hips and sore knees—even my neck hurt from all the impact.

Why? Why did I do this to myself? I didn't even enjoy it. Sure, I sometimes experienced a "runner's high" toward the end of a jog.

But my body constantly felt like I'd been hit by a train, and I had to do an unbelievable amount of mental, physical and caffeinated preparation to gather the energy to hit the pavement. It took no less than a 20-minute pep talk in my head, plus four cups of motor-oil-grade coffee, to acquire even a fraction of the stamina I needed for a 30 minute jog.

On that day three months ago, after I stepped off the scale and then nearly hurled it out a closed window, I couldn't process it. I was unable to wrap my head around how I could work out so hard, sweat so much and be in such physical pain, yet weigh the most I'd ever weighed in my life. And don't give me the "muscle weighs more than fat" argument, because I'd gone up a pants size, too.

Pants. Those sons-a-bitches.

Taking this data, and my pants, into consideration, I examined all my options, I looked at the facts, I thought about the benefits, the drawbacks, and I did it. I came up with this carefully considered, very educated decision:

Fuck you, running.

And so, three months ago, I stopped running, down the road, like an idiot, with *no one* chasing me.

I continued to exercise five days a week, with low-impact cardio like rollerblading, walking or using the elliptical machine, and I lifted weights a few times a week. But running?

Nah. I was done.

And I was done with that damn scale, too.

Or so I said.

Then one day a couple weeks ago, I decided to weigh myself. I'd just got out of bed and hadn't consumed anything yet; I'd *ahem* emptied myself of all fluids and solids, and I was in a really good mood.

It was time to ruin everything by stepping on the scale.

I removed my pajama top, my bottoms, my underwear, my earrings, my bra and my dental fillings. I considered the possibility of removing my arms, maybe my head, but realized I was in the bathroom without any surgical objects—except for a razor. I really didn't think that would do the trick. I took a deep breath and stepped on the scale.

Six pounds gone.

It had to be some kind of mistake. I stepped off the scale and checked the calibration knob. It read "zero." I stepped back on.

Six pounds . . . lost.

I looked up from my feet into the mirror to be sure it was me; I poked myself good and hard in the stomach to ensure I wasn't dreaming. Saw myself, felt the poke. I was conscious, I was me. I was . . .

Six. Pounds. Lighter.

I was also ecstatic. Six measly pounds may not seem that significant, but six pounds on an elf like me is like 15 on a person of normal height.

My pants *had* seemed looser in recent weeks. But I am so used to dieting, exercising and never losing any weight that I figured I was just wearing them too much and stretching out the fabric with my big old ass.

Conveniently naked, and so close to my thinking place, I sat down on the toilet to ponder this. How could it be? How could I struggle so very hard for 30 years to lose weight only to fail repeatedly, and then all of a sudden, lose six pounds in a few months? Without really even trying? What was I doing differently?

Though I'd stopped running, I still exercised, steadily and moderately, and I still ate my regular diet of depressing food: a light breakfast, soup for lunch, vegetables and protein for dinner and a beer in the evening.

That's when it hit me: beer. Of course! For the past few months, I had been drinking really bad beer.

Really, really, *really* bad beer.

It's a new low-calorie beer they just put on the market, one that's half the calories of regular beer. It is perfectly awful. It is absolutely terrible.

It is 55 calories. So I drink it.

A few evenings each week, after my never-ending workday and ridiculous commute, I allow myself the treat of a beer in the evening. Miller Lite, Coors Light—if I was feeling fancy, maybe a Corona with lime.

Of course, the trouble with this, as you know, is that alcohol is fattening.

It is also awesome, after certain stressful things. Have I mentioned my never-ending workday and ridiculous commute?

But still, beer is notoriously bad for the waistline, and during a camping trip in the early summer, my friend Sandy had passed me one of her low-calorie beers when we'd run out of Coors Light.

"Here," she said. "You can have one of mine. It's terrible—tastes like water. But it's beer."

"Thanks!" I said, accepting her generous offer. "I'm sure it will be fine. I'm not very picky about beer."

Sandy smiled knowingly as I popped the top and took a swig.

"Wow," I said, scrunching my face. "This is, like, um . . ."

"Awful? Water? Awful water?" Sandy kept grinning.

I swallowed. "Fine! It's fine! Thank you so much!"

I am nothing if not polite, and again—I'm not very picky about beer.

Somehow, despite my better reasoning, I began buying the awful beer at the store. I did this of my own volition, with no one holding a gun to my head.

And each time I brought it home and took a drink, I had the same internal conversation:

"Wow. This beer sucks . . ."

I took more swigs.

"I mean it really, really sucks . . ."

Toward the end of the bottle:

"Wow. This sucks. Why am I drinking this? I'm done."

Now, after my never-ending workday and ridiculous commute, a few evenings a week, I still have a drink. But I have one. One beer. One and done.

Because it sucks.

I'm glad it sucks. I like this idea of beer that sucks. I wish they'd make food that sucks.

Then again, they do. It's called tofu.

Since that wonderful "Six Pounds Gone!" day a few weeks ago, I've continued the same depressing food/low-impact exercise/crappy beer program and lost five more pounds. The scale continues to creep slowly downward—I no longer feel like heaving it through glass—and my pants, those sons-a-bitches, grow ever looser.

No one has really seemed to notice my weight loss yet; no one has asked me how I've done it.

That's OK. I'll share my secret right here, right now:

Fuck you, running. This body is brought to you by . . .

. . . beer. Really, really, *really* bad beer.

CHAPTER FIFTY
I'm Not a Doctor. I Just Play One in My Marriage
Saturday, 1:14 p.m.

I call it guidance and delegation.

He calls it something else.

So I insist that it's suggesting, requesting and instructing.

But he maintains that it's bitching, nagging and demanding.

Who's right? Have you met me?

Yeah. You know I'm right.

I read WebMD—I know things. And so I always have lots of helpful suggestions for my husband, especially in the realm of health and medicine. I am full of important medical guidance. And stuff.

I love to play doctor for him. Not the naughty game he'd like, but rather my chance to give him lots of healthy advice to ignore, such as:

"Could you please eat something that didn't once have eyes?"

If it hasn't mooed, oinked, clucked or gobbled, he isn't interested. I try, Lord knows I try, to steer him towards the veggies, the fruits, the grains, but in general, he does not dally with food that didn't once have a pulse.

If it ain't bleedin', he ain't eatin'. End of story.

"For shit's sake, wear some sunscreen! I am not changing your Depends when you get skin cancer!"

All good WebMD readers know that religious application of sunscreen is the key to eternal youth, beautiful, cancer-free skin and world peace. He does not read WebMD. He does not know things. He does not apply sunscreen.

I'm stocking up on Depends.

"You don't have to finish the kids' chicken nuggets. You are not the garbage man!"

It is our children's written policy to leave chunks of leftover food on their plates in a carefree manner, thereby wasting money and causing high blood pressure.

But food left on the plates? Not garbage. Not to him.

Where most people would see dirty dishes, the husband sees little meals, and he promptly shoves the leftover food into his mouth. Trash? No. Now, they are snacks.

Aperitifs, if you will.

"Eight cans of Diet Coke does not equal the eight glasses of water you're supposed to drink every day. No wonder you have headaches."

He suffers from headaches, severe headaches, probably once a week. He drinks water, a little bit of water, maybe once every two weeks.

I read WebMD, and I know things, and it says right there that dehydration can cause headaches, and that lack of water causes dehydration. Most of his beverages include caffeine, which is a diuretic and therefore dehydrating. He should drink water. Does he drink water? He does not.

The headaches continue.

Thanks to his lack of listening skills, my husband spends a lot of time suffering from these headaches or just generally feeling ill.

Really, it's a good thing that I'm here to offer suggestions, requests and instructions, because he also flatly refuses to go to the doctor. The man could be on the floor, bleeding from the ears, nose, mouth and belly button, and he would still manage to gurgle:

"I'm fine. No, no—don't call the doctor."

When he's sick and refusing medical treatment like some kind of Old Order Amish man, I always express lots of love and concern, as I did a few minutes ago, when I found him in bed, again, at noon on a Saturday.

"What is wrong with you? Why are you napping *again*?" I ask.

"I have a headache," he replies, covering his eyes.

"You have *another* headache?"

He doesn't move. "I think it's a tumor."

"Well, if it's a tumor, you've had it for 20 years," I tell him.

"It's benign."

"Hmmm . . ." I ponder this "tumor" assertion, coupled with his daily afternoon naps, and flick over to my phone's notes app.

"What are you doing? Taking notes?" he says. "You're going to write about this, aren't you? I'm glad I can be a source of material for you."

"I wish I had your headaches. I want to nap as much as you do . . ."

As I write, I realize that we support each other like this, in sickness, and in health, all the time. He's tossing and turning with illness and fever? I promptly leave. That way he can have the bed to himself. I'm face-forward over the toilet? He chivalrously closes the door, so my noises don't disturb him.

Can't you just feel the love?

From the bed, he continues mumbling.

"Anyway, I may get headaches, but you can't hear," he counters.

"No, *you* can't hear."

Each of us is quite concerned about the other's hearing. He thinks I can't hear. But I know he can't hear. Especially anything I have to say.

"I can hear. You just don't *speak* loud enough," he says.

"What?"

"Blah-blah-blah . . . something . . . something—hearing aids," he says.

Has it occurred to him that, maybe, just perhaps, I don't *want* to hear what he has to say?

Yes, sometimes he tries to turn the tables and play doctor with me, offering dubious medical guidance and suggestions.

For some reason, I just can't hear him.

The joke's on him, though. I've grown tired of not listening to his babble. So, unbeknownst to him, a few weeks ago I scheduled an appointment with the audiologist and had my ears checked.

Guess what? As it turns out, my hearing is perfectly normal. But that is no surprise to me. I figured as much.

I read WebMD. I know things.

CHAPTER FIFTY-ONE
He Didn't Even Buy Me a Drink First
Monday, 10:50 a.m.

He says I'm special. But that's not why I let him get to third base.

And beyond.

He's my gynecologist, and he likes tell me that I am truly extraordinary now, because I've unwillingly joined his elite "Over 40 Club." This entitles me to a very specific exam that's as pleasant as getting stabbed, only worse. And I'm not referring to him poking around in my Virginia, no—I'm referring to the exam I now endure in my back door, my log launcher . . .

. . . my butt.

Doc says he has to do it, has to check the old chute for growths, tumors, turtles, Bart Simpson—hell, I don't know what he's looking for in there. I just know that for the past four or five years, he goes where no man has gone before, and he sticks his finger in my starfish, my Gary . . .

. . . my butt.

I keep hoping he'll forget. But no, he never does. He paws my boobs, probes around my love canal and next thing I know, whoomp, there it is, his finger in my bullet-hole, my brown-eye, my butt.

With exams like that, you'd think I'd remember it, but my annual gyno appointment takes me by surprise every time. This year, it fell on September 1, which is normally a happy day for me because it signifies the annual Packing Away of the Razor, as I generally don't shave during months that end in "-ber" or "-ary."

Though it is early in the season, I already have tons of personal grooming to address. I really need to shave my, um, legs. The doctor will certainly not be able to see much unless I really get in there and shave my, um, legs properly.

The appointment means several other things too, none of them good: I won't let myself eat or drink anything for hours, as I know I'll have to step on the evil medical scale. And even though I've been following my diet of disappointing food and Really Bad Beer, and have recently lost 12 pounds according to *my* scale, I know I'll weigh five to 10 pounds more at the doctor's office, because I *always* weigh five to 10 pounds more at the doctor's office.

I hate that fucking medical scale.

Short of canceling the appointment, which they'd charge me for, there is nothing I can do about it, and anyway, I've gone through the whole thing several times before. I fix a cup of coffee and resign myself to the fact that my annual anal violation will ensue in an hour. I definitely need that time— and more. For the arduous process of shaving my, um, legs.

So I shower, shave my, um, legs and drive to town; I park the car, sign the sheet and sit down. Soon enough, the nurse calls me to the back hallway, and says the three dreaded words:

"Let's weigh you."

I follow her to the fucking medical scale, slide off my shoes and prepare for the worst. Little do I know, the worst is not to be my weight.

She pulls out the height bar. "Let's just measure you first."

Well, she doesn't have to waste her time—I know the answer to that. "I'm 5'2"," I tell her, "and a *half.*"

"Mm-hmm," she mumbles. Personality is not her strong point. She angles the metal over my head. "You're 5'1."

"What?!"

She looks up from her chart, and levels her gaze at me. "I *said*, you're 5'1.'"

"No, no. That's not right. I'm 5'2—*and a half,* actually!" I tell her. "Measure me again. Please."

The nurse barely stifles an eye-roll as she sighs and pulls the bar back over my head. "Five. One. See?" she points to the numbers. "Five. Foot. One."

I squint at the metallic measurements on the ruler, and see that the bar undeniably rests at 5'1". I've been 5'2"—*and a half*—since I turned 15, but apparently, at age 44, I have already begun shrinking. Lovely. Great news! What next?

She slides the scale's bottom weight to 100, and begins the top bar's ascent up, up, up the line, until it rests at, well, none of your business, but four pounds heavier than I do at home, embarrassingly high for a mere woman of 5'1."

I tell you, I hate that fucking medical scale.

Still, as I watch No-Personality Nurse write down the wholly inaccurate numbers, I feel pretty good. Even with the alleged shrinkage and four-pound variance over my home scale, I can see by my medical chart that I've definitely lost 12 pounds since my last visit.

I follow Nurse Ratched into exam room three, feigning attention to her droned instruction for the robe and lap blanket. She leaves, I change into the thin paper, and while climbing onto the table I notice several new, colorful signs on the walls:

"Botox! Available here!"

"Age spots? Dark patches? Look years younger with our Sciton laser!"

"Shed unwanted pounds! Ask Doctor Miller about his new weight loss program!"

Huh. Have I wandered into my gynecologist's office, or a plastic surgeon's office? Someone has their heads and tails mixed up. Either that, or Dr. Miller has begun offering beauty services, and I wouldn't put it past him. He's always seemed a free-thinking, spunky sort as well as kind of . . .

"HELLOOOOOOO!!"

. . . loud.

He bursts through the door, all white coat and dark hair, chattering in exclamation points and somehow simultaneously tapping on the laptop folded in the crook of his arm.

"Dawn! How are we doing? Any medical changes?!"

My ears begin to ring, and just the sight of him causes my blood pressure to rise and my rear end to *clench*.

"No, doc, everything's fine," I say.

"Any pain with intercourse?! Any abnormal bleeding?!"

Clench. "Nope. None of that."

He nods, still typing on his computer. "So! What's new with you?"

"Well," I say, "I'm afraid there's been some kind of terrible mistake. I've always been 5'2"—*and a half*—but your nurse out there says I'm 5'1" today. Your height measurer/medical scale thingie must be off."

He puts his laptop down, picks up my chart and flips through the pages. "No, no!" he shouts. "It's very accurate! What happens is, as we age . . ."

Oh, here we go. Another "As we age" speech. These are becoming more and more common since I joined the "Over 40 Club." In them, doc relays the wonderful changes I should expect in my breasts, my menstrual cycle, my mood—not to mention my colon.

Clench.

" . . . and we can expect to shrink as much as two inches in our lifetimes!"

I zone back in as he fiddles with my chart.

"Hmm," he points at something. "The insurance companies want us to tell patients now when they're overweight, and at 5'1", the BMI table says you should weigh about three pounds less!"

Yeah. I have a feeling it's Dr. Miller and his handy "Weight Loss

Program!" who really want me to know I am a whopping three pounds overweight. I don't quite know what to say to his blatant pitch, so I do what I always do in such situations: I smile. I nod. I smile and nod.

"Go ahead and lie back now!"

Ah, time for him to take his annual walk through my lady garden. Good thing I shaved my, um, legs.

He chatters on as he rounds second base, then paws his way down to third, giving me a clean bill of health in the old swimsuit areas. Suddenly, he stops and looks up, staring fixedly at my face.

"You really have some age spots starting there, on your cheeks and forehead," he says, tilting his head. "We have that new Sciton laser. It'll take off 10 years!"

Wow.

I came into the gynecologist's office feeling good, fit and 5'2"—*and a half.*

I'll be leaving the gynecologist's office short, fat, apparently ancient—and carrying a pamphlet for beauty treatments.

I shaved my, um, legs for this?

He sits between my knees, still looking at my face, or my age spots, hard to tell, as if expecting a reply.

I smile. I nod. I smile and nod. "OK. Thanks for letting me know."

"No problem!" he says. "It's just part of what we do around here for all you ladies in the Over 40 Club!" He winks and returns his attentions down south.

And, without further ado, he sticks his finger in my balloon knot, my prison purse . . .

. . . my butt.

Clench.

CHAPTER FIFTY-TWO
Mother Got a Smartphone. Cussing Ensued
Tuesday, 12:34 p.m.

One phone call.

That's all it takes to wreck my day, screw up my plans and strike fear into my very soul. That's all it takes to send me barreling off the track of busy, contented productivity and straight into an abyss of frustration, profanity, confusion and exasperation.

What is it? What could possibly be that bad? Layoff? Bankruptcy? Zombie apocalypse?

Nope. One phone call, that's all it is, relaying this horrifying news:

Mother got a smartphone.

Please. Send help. Or Xanax.

At age 70, Mom is a kind, funny, smart woman, but the intricacies of modern technology elude her. She's just wholly unable to navigate complex technological equipment, such as the power button of her TV remote.

For 25 years, this woman served as a registered nurse, supervising an entire hospital unit with dozens of patients simultaneously under her care. Many times, on her commute to and from work, she stopped at roadside accidents and administered critical first aid.

Are you sick? Bleeding? Having a heart attack? Mom's your girl; she can save your life. But if you need her to turn on a computer?

You're out of luck.

Several times a month, township police speed to her residence for burglar alarm notifications. There, they find her punching angrily at the electronic ADT keypad as a decibel-defying siren blares in the background.

Cussing ensues.

We got her a laptop a few years ago. She was initially thrilled, but now it sits, dusty and abandoned, because she's forgotten how to turn it on. Thinking she needed something simpler, I bought her a tablet last Christmas. She loved it—at first. Now it sits, dusty and abandoned, because she's forgotten how to turn it on.

We will not speak of the flat-screen TVs, the color printers, the DVD players she's purchased on her own. But I'm willing to bet that they're sitting, dusty and abandoned, because she's forgotten how to turn them on.

The difficult part of all this is that I serve as Mom's—and for that matter, my entire family's—Freak Squad. I am the reluctant, dubious, completely free alternative to Best Buy's Geek Squad. I unpack the computers, plug them in and install the software. I set up the printers, wire the televisions, defrag the hard drives, run speaker wire, and initialize many a PlayStation and Wii.

And that was just on Saturday.

Most families have a Freak Squad member. Some fool like me who has the little bit of smarts it takes to put the yellow plug into the yellow hole. Or click "Next" every three seconds until the software works.

Sure, Freak Squad members have other names. "Suckers" comes to mind. "Doormats" works. Also "chumps" seems to fit.

This particular Freak Squad member does plenty of her customer care via telephone, and a large percentage of it for her mother; hence you can imagine the horror I'm feeling now, as I see my mother's landline number pop up on my screen.

I brace myself. "Hello?"

"This Goddamn thing!"

Cussing has ensued. Freak Squad time.

"What'd you buy, Mom?"

"A new #%*&^**# cell phone!"

"What kind of cell phone, Mom?"

"It's one of those . . . those #%*&^**# smartphones! With the little robot on it!"

Oh, no. An Android phone. My heart sinks; this is bad, truly awful news. I slump back into my chair to endure what likely will require at least a 45-minute conversation.

When Mom deals with technology, cussing ensues at ear-splitting decibels. To prevent further hearing loss, I lower my phone volume, so I only catch the tail end of what she says next.

". . . and I've been trying all #%*&^**# morning to get it activated, but it won't do it! It won't activate!"

"Does it tell you why?" I ask. "Usually, it gives you some kind of reason or error message."

"I don't think so!" she yells. "It just keeps saying something about 'airplane mode!'"

Airplane mode. That's an easy fix—just a quick setting to change and she'll be good to go. Maybe this will be a short customer care call.

"Well, that's your problem right there, Mom," I say. "Your phone won't work when it's in airplane mode."

"It won't work at all until I activate it!"

I lean forward onto my desk and put my head in my hands.

"There's a setting you need to change, Mom. You need to . . ."

"IT WON'T WORK UNTIL I ACTIVATE IT!"

It is time to fight shouty capitals with shouty capitals.

"MOM!" I holler. "It WILL NOT ACTIVATE until you take it out of AIRPLANE MODE! Airplane mode CUTS OFF THE PHONE'S SIGNAL so you can play games and what-not on an airplane WITHOUT CAUSING SIGNAL INTERFERENCE FOR THE PILOT! Your phone CAN'T ACTIVATE without a signal TO THE SATELLITE!"

I collapse back in my chair, out of breath. I feel guilty for raising my voice, but I know from past experience that sometimes it's the only way to get through.

"Oh!" she says. "Well, how do I get it out of airplane mode?"

"OK," I reply. "I can help you do that. Go to settings."

"Where's settings?"

"Go to your home screen."

"Where's the home screen?"

I put my head down on my desk, and pound my forehead on its surface. I am almost out of patience.

Still, we are close. If I can just power through, I'll navigate her to the home screen, she'll find the settings and turn off airplane mode and be good to go.

"To get to your home screen, you just tap that little house icon."

"What's an icon?"

And . . . that does it. Freak Squad fail. I fold.

It has become crystal clear that her technological problems reside far beyond the realm of my meager abilities. She needs to call the cell phone company. It will be an interesting conversation, because Mom speaks in cuss words and exclamation points, and tech support people, in general, no habla Ingles.

I wish them well.

"Mom. I'm three hours away, and I can't help you with this because I can't be there to show you," I say. "You're going to have to call the cell phone company."

Cussing ensues.

"I don't want to call those #%*&^**#!!" she yells.

I try to make her feel better. "At least your new phone will have unlimited text, and you can send me messages!"

"#%*&^**#!!" she replies.

"When you get through and have it all hooked up, be sure and send me a text message so I have your new number!"

"#%*&^**#!! . . ."

"Love you! Bye!"

I still feel somewhat guilty, but I have to get back to work. Also, I have grown deaf.

You might say, "That's your mom, not you. The cell phone company can help. Those are her problems—not yours."

Oh, young grasshopper—sorry, but you're wrong. Did you learn nothing from therapy?

Mother's problems are *always* our problems.

And I'm still waiting on that text.

CHAPTER FIFTY-THREE
1996 Called. It Wants Its Phone Back
Thursday, 6:49 a.m.

The husband has a crackhead phone.

Actually, along with your average bums, thugs and pimps, crackheads own better phones than he does, judging by the hooligans I see on the streets of downtown Columbus, filthy and shifty and chatting languidly on their iPhones.

He claims his device is fine and says he doesn't even want a phone, let alone a smartphone. The only reason my spouse owns a cell phone at all is because I foisted it on him as a Christmas gift five years ago—a good four years after everyone else in the world owned cell phones, including his 79-year-old mom.

It was a heavy responsibility, being the wife of the last remaining American without a cell phone, so when I finally made the decision to buy him one, I researched it thoroughly, finding a cheap, no-contract model. I also made sure it was extremely easy to use, as my spouse doesn't have much in the way of technological expertise. "Guess what I learned to do today! I saved a file in Word!" is his idea of computer mastery.

So I chose cheaply and carefully and five years ago, on Christmas morning, I wrapped the little Obama-phone up and placed it under the tree. I could barely contain my excitement as I handed him my thoughtful, yet entirely sensible, present.

He was so appreciative.

"Oh, now why did you buy me this?" he asked, frowning. "I don't need a cell phone!"

I tried to remain calm. Tried. "Because, honey—everyone has cell phones now. *Your mom* has a cell phone."

"But I don't need one!"

I took a deep breath. "Yes, you do. You have two young children, and we both work an hour away from them in the city each day. You need a phone!"

"Not me—I'm just a regular guy," he said, puffing up his flannel-shirted chest. "I'm a . . . simple man!"

At that point, I had to turn away and hand out the rest of the presents to the kids. When he starts quoting Lynyrd Skynyrd, which he does—often—I have the urge to hit him.

Over the head.

With a chair.

He grumbled and complained as he removed the phone's packaging. He grumbled and complained as I set it up. He grumbled and complained as my daughter showed him how to use it.

But slowly, almost imperceptibly, over these five years, the Regular Guy learned to use, then tolerate, then perhaps even like his crappy pre-paid crackhead phone.

In fact, I'm starting to think he's in a relationship with it, because he won't give it up. The thing is dying an ugly death: He can't send pictures anymore; he can't receive MMS or any group texts. When he slides the device open, its hinges creak like a crypt, and chunks of plastic fall to the floor.

Perhaps more troublesome is that he no longer can see the phone's numbers and letters. He's aged in the decade or two since receiving it, and now requires reading glasses to read small print. This, combined with the fact that his phone's screen measures about 1.5 inches, leads to an interesting and comical scene every time he tries to read or send a text.

That's how I found him last week, squinting and cussing and punching furiously at the tiny keypad. I walked over and rested my hand on his shoulder. "Honey," I said. "It's time."

"Time for what?" Still laboring over a message, he didn't look up at me.

"It's time for you to let that thing go," I replied. "It's falling apart. Anyway, you need a smartphone. How about a nice iPhone?" I quickly appeased his miser side. "Not the brand new one. Like last year's model."

"I don't need any damn expensive smartphone!" he grumbled.

"Smartphones have been around for years," I tried to reason with him. I tried. "They've come way down in price. You're a police officer. You call *me* to Google addresses for you—on *my smartphone!*"

He shook his head and mumbled, but kept his attentions on the laborious task at hand. The discussion was closed, I could tell, and for the time being, I gave up.

I just didn't get it. As I said, I use my phone for just about everything these days: writing, taking photos, surfing the web, reading on the toilet . . .

very important tasks. So I don't understand someone who chooses *not* to have a smartphone. That's like choosing not to be happy. That's like choosing pain over pleasure.

That's like going without liquids for three days, then finally being offered a huge glass of ice water only to reply, "No thanks. I'll just go ahead and die."

He treats us, his family, like gold. It can take some time, but the kids and I are able to talk him into buying us just about anything with a bit of charm, sweet-talk and sometimes, chocolate.

When it comes to things for him, it's an entirely different story and truly, sometimes I think I married an Amish dude. The guy has owned the same few flannel shirts since college, tops so raggedy and thin that they have the thread-count of a gauze first-aid pad. He will cheerfully wear old underwear until they are crotchless.

And not in any kind of fun way.

Luckily, I have a plan. He is getting a smartphone this year, and he's going to like it.

Eventually.

But I know how it'll all go down on Christmas Day. Again.

"Oh, now why did you buy me this?" he'll protest. "I don't need a smartphone!"

He will grumble and complain as he removes its packaging. He will grumble and complain as I set it up. He will grumble and complain as my daughter shows him how to use it. And I will try to be patient with him. I'll try.

"I don't need this," he'll say. "I'm just a regular guy. I'm a simple man!"

Simple, huh? True enough. But in the end, the Simple Man/Regular Guy/Amish Husband will just have to adapt. It's time. Because, like I said, *everyone* has smartphones these days. His mom has a smartphone. Hell—my mom has a smartphone.

Even the crackheads have smartphones.

CHAPTER FIFTY-FOUR
I'm Not Bossy. I'm Just a Born Leader
Friday, 7:56 p.m.

It's almost 8 p.m.—the witching hour. I've been home since 7, but the kids have just arrived back from sports practices. I heard them come in the kitchen and throw their backpacks on the table. They're plowing around, looking for junk food.

I better go out there, provide some parental guidance, maybe direct them to the fruits and vegetables.

I do so, and then return to the bedroom, a.k.a. the husband's "office," where he is kicked back, relaxing.

"I think you enjoy that," he says.

I pull off my shirt and begin changing into pajamas. "Enjoy what?"

"Nagging the kids when they get home," he replies. "You sure are bossy."

"I am not bossy," I shoot back. "I'm just . . . exhibiting leadership skills. Anyway, if I don't go out there, all hell breaks loose. Nobody eats vegetables, nobody takes baths, nobody does their chores." I pause to watch him as he stares vacantly into the TV, lounging back and eating a cookie. In the bed. On the sheets I just changed. "Yeah. I'd like to live in your world."

He nods. "It's pretty nice. You'd like it. There's cookies," he pauses thoughtfully and looks over at my chest, "and lovin' once or twice a week."

"What do you mean 'lovin'? We weren't even talking about that!"

"Yeah," he says. "But I was thinking about it."

He has a filthy mind.

He also has a point. I do tend to cram much of my helpful guidance into a very small window of time. I have to. With my work schedule and the kids' school and sports activities, I only really see them for an hour before bedtime each night. And all day at work, I use texting to stay in contact. I send them loving messages such as:

Fold the laundry, you lazy Princess!

Brush your teeth, you stinky Hobo!

Put your dishes in the dishwasher, you little hooligans!

They never respond to my texts. I have no idea why.

Luckily, technology has brought us a new way to communicate. My kids don't know it yet, but I've just figured out that I can use the video chat app to talk to them face-to-face and offer more guidance when I'm not with them.

They will be thrilled about this.

So am I! Now, in an immediate and very personal manner, I can provide the kind of leadership that my children have come to expect from me, even when I'm far away. With just a few quick taps on this phone, I'll be able to dial them up, see their sweet faces and give them plenty of counsel.

Another reason I'm so stoked about this video technology is that my poor kids seem to have trouble with their eyes. Oh sure, they can see me and everything else on the screens of their cell phones and iPods, but they seem to be blind to certain other things, and with video chat, I'll be able to help them locate what they just can't see on their own.

For instance, with this technology, I can point out all the healthy foods waiting in the kitchen, available for their consumption. When I'm not home to force fruits and vegetables upon them in my usual fashion, I can direct them to the grapes, the lettuce, the bananas—foods they couldn't seem to find before.

And I will be able to suggest certain acts of hygiene in which they should engage. The Hobo especially needs help in this area, and with this new-fangled cell phone camera magic, I can guide him to the hairbrush, the toothpaste and especially, the bathtub.

The kids also suffer from terrible vision problems, and possibly amnesia, when it comes to their papers, backpacks and the kitchen table. Items are left, forgotten, strewn about. Now, with a simple click of a button, I can look past their darling heads and see all sorts of things they've left behind: the laundry, dirty dishes, books, my sanity.

I'm not the first Weber to understand the benefits of technology, no; the children have long used it to their advantage. Several evenings a week, they log on for a vigorous dose of online shopping: Amazon, GameStop.com, Abercrombie.com. Decisions are made. Items are listed. Virtual shopping carts are filled. At night, when I arrive home from work, 17-page lists printed with ink costing $57 per milliliter are shoved in my hand before I even put my purse away. Then I know what I can buy for them that particular day.

Isn't that thoughtful? And all accomplished with such diligence! Such attention to detail!

I'm really glad they take the initiative to find solutions, because they have a dreadful, serious problem.

They're bored.

Tragic, no? The little lambs find their world so very dull. It's truly a difficult life they lead. Every day is a struggle.

But with this video chat, I can help them by pointing out such possessions as: 159 video games on three different systems, a dog, a trampoline, two computers, an iPhone, an iPod, five bikes, hundreds of DVDs, and an in-ground damn swimming pool.

And if they're *still* bored, I'll just direct them to the unfolded laundry, the dirty dishes, the books and bags strewn all over the place. They will be thrilled about this. So am I. Better nagging through technology, that's what I always say.

CHAPTER FIFTY-FIVE
There's an App for That. Yes—That
Sunday, 2:11 p.m.

It has, um, come to my attention that the list of things this smartphone can do includes . . .

. . . me.

And just when I thought it was safe to borrow someone else's cell phone, I will now run, terrified and screaming, away from that idea until I find the nearest vat of bleach.

Perhaps I should explain. There I was a few minutes ago, bored, minding my own—you know, just living out my life of quiet desperation, when I decided I should maybe do some meaningful work here on my phone.

So I pulled up Google's Android Market, "Play," to download a few useful, productive apps, such as "Bike Race" and "Subway Surfer."

That's when I found this:

"Sexy Vibes"

And then I ran, terrified and screaming, in search of a vat of bleach.

It appears people can download "Sexy Vibes," turn it, um, on, and rub their actual cell phones on their actual personal regions.

Truly, the end of days is nigh.

Mobile phones have always had a "vibrate" mode for calls, but thanks to the creators of apps like "Sexy Vibes," the function can be switched on for as long as needed, or until a, um, "goal" is achieved.

Yes, folks are now using cell phones to baste their turkey, to abuse their fuse. They're patting the bunny, double-clicking the mouse, five-finger shuffling, getting a little me-time—with their phones.

Let me repeat that so it sinks in: PEOPLE ARE MASTURBATING

WITH THEIR PHONES.

Things of this nature are enough to send an OCD germophobe like me, terrified and screaming, over the edge. Please tell me—what causes a reasonably sane person to look at a phone in such an, um, amorous manner? Jim Morrison was wrong; people aren't strange.

People are fucking weird. And they're getting weirder all the time.

I will admit that I can see one advantage to a cell-phone vibrator app: the recharge-ability factor. I may or may not have a "friend" who, um, may or may not possess an entire drawer full of marital aids, all of which she may or may not be able to use because the batteries are dead.

And these aren't just any batteries, she tells me, these aren't just double-As; these are the itty-bitty, son-of-a-bitch specialized electronic batteries, the ones that all look the same but have numbers like "CR209-OMGFU-7." She always forgets to remove the batteries and put them in my, er, her purse, in order to find replacements at the store.

That's what "she" tells me, anyway.

I figured my other pals would be similarly amused/disgusted by "Sexy Vibes," and I was right. As always, the ladies did not let me down.

My friends' reactions ran the gamut from customer-driven:

"Talk about great phone service!" said Mari.

To declarations of devotion:

"I've often said I love my smartphone more than I should love a thing," commented Beth. "But I didn't know it could love me back."

To jealousy amongst gadgets:

"Great," wrote Gaynell, "now my shower massager will be jealous of my cell phone."

To location, location, location:

"Now I know why some women keep their phones in their front pocket," said Robin.

To smartphone shunning:

"I will never ask to see someone's cell phone again," said Sarah.

Me neither, Sarah, me neither.

I did a little more online research—that is just the kind of investigative journalist I am—and I found more than 110 other vibrator programs on Google "Play," most costing around 99 cents: "Epic Vibrator," "Smart Vibrator," "Fun Vibrator," "Magic Vibrator," "Vibrator Dildo." There's also the plain vanilla "Vibrator: Classic," the very promising "Epic Vibrator," and the aptly named, "Zing Zing Wing Wing (Vibrator)." And, iPhone users rejoice, for you also have several choices, including "iBrateVibrate," "iVibe Massager" and the plain but capable-sounding "Sex Toy."

As with all apps, Google "Play" members can leave feedback on these utilities. Dozens of user/geniuses wrote a variety of badly misspelled, moronic observations.

Commenters ranged from jealous boyfriends:

"My girlfriend likes my Android phone more than me! I feel so jealous of my Android! Dammit!"

To, um, gushing devotees:

"Im in lov, daam (sic)! Absolutely fabulace (sic)! God I feel so alive! Who needs men!"

To the hygienically concerned:

"Wow. I love it. I put it in a little baggie!"

To future traffic fatalities:

"I use it all the time when I'm driving! All u have to do is slide up and down on ur phone."

To West Virginians:

"This app sucks. waste of time, I accidentally penis-dialed my grandmother."

Sigh. I try not to judge—I am not a prude. I mean, who hasn't snuck a peek at porn? Who hasn't considered the possibilities of the vibrating chair?

Who among us doesn't have a drawer full of sex toys with dead, itty-bitty, son-of-a-bitch batteries?

Oh. That's just me?

But for all my garden-variety knowledge and perviness and drawer full of, um, dead "massagers," I have never, ever glanced at a Motorola with a gleam in my eye. Anyway, I don't know about you, but I lose my phone enough. I don't need to misplace it in the metaphorical deep end.

OK. I'm done. I'll get off my dirty digital soapbox.

But in the meantime, I'm here to help all the geniuses over at Google "Play": I can save all of you randy bastards 99 cents, because you don't require any of these apps. Tell me, Einsteins: Are you lonely? Bereft? Just flat-out horny? Do you miss your spouse, your partner, your lover? You don't need "Sexy Vibes," "Vibrator: Classic" or "Epic Vibrator." You don't even need "Zing Zing Wing Wing: Vibrator." Just have someone, preferably not your grandmother (unless you're a West Virginian), call you. In vibrate mode, repeatedly, or until your, um, "goal" is achieved.

Well, I sure am happy to bring you this hard-hitting journalism. I think we've all learned something here, and it is: On this planet, there is no end to the many and various things that people will attempt to hump.

And some folks really love their phones.

In the biblical sense.

Apparently.

CHAPTER FIFTY-SIX
My Friends Got to Meet Dave Barry and All I Got Was Cheap Beer
Saturday, 8:38 p.m.

All I want from him is a picture, maybe a signature, possibly a hug.

All he'll ever want from me is a restraining order.

Dave Barry: my favorite published author. At last count, I owned 23 of his books. I collect them like postage stamps, read them like a fiend and study them like textbooks.

Don't ask me what I'd say to Dave Barry if I ever met him. The truth is, I have encountered a few celebrities, and I always manage to make a blithering idiot of myself by either:

1. Gaping at them in open-mouthed shock (The Aretha Franklin Elevator Incident), or;

2. Gaping at them in open-mouthed shock, and then shouting, "Holy shit!" (The Peter Gabriel Backstage Incident)

I shouldn't worry about it, because the truth is that Dave Barry and I will probably never meet. Still, I often fantasize that we'll bump into each other at some writer's event. He'll read my work, set me up with his agent and we'll become best writer buddies.

The more likely scenario (The Pending Dave Berry Incident): I'd gape at him in open-mouthed shock, and shout "Holy shit!"

I had a chance to stalk, um, swear at, er, meet Dave Barry, tonight, at the National Society of Newspaper Columnists (NSNC) conference in Hartford, Connecticut. I write a surprisingly cuss-word free humor column for the local paper, and in 2011, I won an NSNC award for it. No one is sure how this happened.

I attended the 2011 conference in Detroit to pick up my award, but because of finances, I haven't been able to attend the annual conferences since then.

My kids' iPhones don't buy themselves.

People, I have a tip for you: When it's a lovely Saturday night like tonight, and you're feeling really blue because you can't afford to stalk your favorite author at a conference, by all means—go ahead. Pull up Facebook on your phone. There, you'll find dozens of pictures of writer friends, all having tons of fun at said conference and mingling with said author, who seems down-to-earth and cool enough to hang out and tolerate tons of gratuitous photos.

Hahaha—good times! I feel the urge to, as my friend Rick says, "cut myself with a plastic knife from Wendy's."

But I don't. I avoid the utensil drawer and go looking for the husband, whom I find in his "office" (the bed), doing what he calls "work" (watching *American Pickers* and scratching himself).

"I'm sad," I tell him. Even though he is, um, working, I hope to parlay my misery into a night on the town.

I am not one to miss an opportunity.

"Whatsa matter?" he pulls his eyes from the television to me.

"Well, my writer friends are hanging out with Dave Barry at the NSNC conference, taking pictures with him and hugging him and having a great time," I say. "Look at all these photos on Facebook!"

I flash the phone his way, and he squints at my screen.

"Who's Dave Berries?"

"It's Dave *Barry*!" I yell. "Next to Erma, he's, like, the best humor writer ever! Haven't you seen all those books of his I have in the basement? That one entire shelf? I knew I should have gone to the conference. I knew it."

He holds out his arms. "Aw—come here, baby. I'll be your Dave Barry."

Hoping for a little comfort—and maybe an expensive dinner—I shuffle over to him. Hugging ensues. Groping ensues. Attempted fondling of my swimsuit areas ensued.

He is not one to miss an opportunity.

"Um, Dave Barry is married," I say, pulling away. "I don't think he'd try to touch me there."

I mope out of the bedroom, wondering how to make myself feel better. But I realize that it is Saturday night, with or without Dave Barry, and I still have some 12-ounce cans of "feel better" in the fridge. I grab a couple of them, and head over to see my neighbor, Wise Marj.

Wise Marj has a six-pack of feel better in the fridge herself, she always does—as I've said, I call her Wise Marj for a reason—and she pulls them out, along with a bag of salt and vinegar chips. In two bright red Adirondack chairs, we commence feeling better by complaining about finances, grousing about work and grumbling about spouses. Marj's smelly and extremely cheerful dog, Lucky, wags around and rests his very large, very pungent head in our laps, and sniffs our feet, hopeful, as always, for a dropped chip.

A while later, the phone pings with a text:

"Hi, I'm Dave Berries. I've heard so much about u from ur friends and love ur articles wish I could have met u hopefully next year :)"

Huh. Imagine that. "Dave Berries" and the husband share the same phone number.

I text him back:

"Dave 'Berries' ur an ass. An adorable ass, but an ass nonetheless."

While on the phone, I flip back over to Facebook, where upsetting NSNC pictures continue to drop through my newsfeed; Dave Barry, it seems, will let anyone take a picture with him. There's Dave Barry with my friend Stacey, Dave Barry with Robert, Dave Barry with some homeless guy.

But no Dave Barry with Dawn.

Depressing.

"Look at this," I flash Marj the phone. "All my writer friends are hanging out in Hartford, partying with Dave Barry, and I'm in Ohio, drinking canned beer and eating stinky chips with you."

She squints at the photos. "Who's Dave Berries?"

Good grief. I roll my eyes, then turn to watch the orange ball of sun sink below the horizon. Before long, Wise Marj and I are down to our last drops.

Beer: drank. Chips: gone. Feeling: not much better, but it is time to go.

We stand, pick up our cans and crumble the chip bag as Lucky, ever happy, ever hopeful, investigates the chairs for remnants. I plod home.

And there, I find one "Dave Berries," sleeping after a busy day of "work" in his "office." I stare at him for a minute as he snores and drools in the blinking blue glow of *American Pickers*, then smile, shake my head, and climb under the covers.

Dave Berries is no Dave Barry.

But I'll take what I can get. Reality is never a concern for me.

Dave Berries will have to do.

EPILOGUE
No Bears, No Pants, No Problems
Thursday, 8:25 p.m.

I am camping. By myself. You know, as one does.

Let's just look at that for a minute because I know what you're picturing: a middle-aged elfin blonde woman crouched over a single flame in the deep, dark woods, eating beans from a can and using leaves for personal hygiene. You see me shivering, scared, alone, and developing a rash due to bad leaf choices.

You are horrified.

You're not the only one. When I told friends and family I'd planned a solo camping trip, they stared at me in open-mouthed shock, like I'd volunteered for a root canal, or perhaps signed up for active duty in Iraq.

"You mean you're camping *by yourself?*"

"Aren't you afraid?"

"Won't you be bored?"

The answers to the above are yes, no and HELL no, but still they remained aghast. At work, my buddy Al was especially concerned.

"You better be careful," he said, wrinkling his brow. "Watch out for bears!"

I tried to ease his mind by pointing out that I'd be staying in a highly rated modern campground with running water, wifi and absolutely zero bears, but he remained unconvinced.

"Take your phone," he said. "Take some mace!"

Of course I brought my phone because A) it's pretty much attached to my hand at all times, and B) the whole reason for the trip is to find quiet writing time to finish this book. To that end, I packed my bags, printer and several chargers, and the husband dropped me off at a glorious, magical place where I'd be able to write somewhere other than behind the locked door of a bathroom.

And no one needs to worry, as I don't camp—I glamp, warm and safe from strangers, the elements and all manner of bears. After the Stupid Camping trip of '07, the husband and I purchased a travel trailer, and this is how we roll now: 27 feet of heated luxury. Nicer than any of my single years apartments, our "glamper" has air conditioning, a comfortable queen-size bed, and for some odd reason, an oven. Best of all, this baby has a toilet. That flushes. Flushes especially well at 1 a.m. And 3 a.m. And sometimes 5:30 a.m.

Ah, flushing. You complete me. Literally.

I've been here for four days, writing, editing and doing things I normally don't get to do, such as sitting in silence for a full five minutes. I've watched chick flicks on DVD, drank the occasional glass of wine, and cooked all manner of healthy, stinky food. Salmon, blue cheese, sautéed mushrooms— if it smells bad and my kids hate it, I've been eating it.

Not only that, my solo exile also means I get to participate in my favorite pastime of not wearing pants. I lounge around the camper in underwear and a t-shirt, happily engaging in such pants-free activities as sleeping, eating and watching television with the help of a small and amazing gadget I haven't had in my hand for 20-plus years. A remote control, I think it's called, and why, it couldn't be more wonderful. Did you know, for example, that *a female* can actually use this device? To change the channel? Did you know that there are programs on television besides college football and *American Pickers*?

I did not.

And thanks to the lack of spouse, the nightly decibel level in bed has lowered by approximately 40 points, which means I can sleep. Why, several times in a row, aside from my geezer bathroom breaks, I slept all the way through the night, and one morning, I slept until 8:47 a.m. Like some kind of normal person!

Now, it's not all rainbows and unicorns and uninterrupted sleep. The weather's been cold and rainy, but since I'm here to write, this actually works in my favor. I park myself inside at the table, glancing up only occasionally to look through wet windows. I'm not missing a thing.

Or at least, I thought I wasn't. In the spare moments between writing, eating smelly food and basically just enjoying myself, I get a weird feeling. A nagging feeling. It took me a while to figure out why. But earlier tonight, everything became clear.

I'd decided to take a bath. I was excited to do so. I don't always approach bathing with such enthusiasm, mostly because all I usually have time for is a brief shower with the Hobo's Spiderman toy and the two gallons of hot water the Princess leaves in the tank. So the prospect of slipping into a tub of warm water and having 15 minutes of comfort was pretty thrilling, and even though I'd have to fold my body in two to get into the twee camper tub, I looked forward to it as I peeled off my clothes and sank gratefully into sudsy, action figure-free water. I washed slowly, listened to Pandora, sipped a nice a glass of boxed wine, and tried to relax and enjoy the moment.

I tried, that is. As I've said before, I do not know the thing called "relaxation." Something just felt off. Something felt amiss. When I rose from the tub and reached for the hook, I realized what was gone.

The wet towel.

Indeed, the towel I grabbed and wrapped around my body felt bone dry. Without the husband there to steal it and use it on his hairy man regions, I had a clean, lovely lady-towel, completely unmolested. I didn't know quite what to do with such a luxury. And there in the tiny trailer bathroom, with only the wind and rain for company, I realized this is how it could be someday. No wet towel. No cold water. No Spiderman at all. Just me.

The husband and I each started our adult lives the way most people do: living single, one person rattling around in a house. Then there were two, which led, of course, to three and four. I know those numbers will someday, hopefully years from now, go backward—four, three, two, one—and *I love you. Now go away* will become *I love you. Please don't go.*

Finished bathing, I sit now at the camper table waiting for my hair to dry. I'll head back in the morning and I admit it—I've enjoyed myself. I enjoyed the freedom; I enjoyed the ability to think in peace and tap my thoughts out while sitting somewhere besides bleachers or the bathroom. It's been a fantastic four-day writing fest, a pants-free, bra-free and entirely bear-free solo glamping trip. But as much as I'd wanted to get away, I'm not sure who I am if I'm not being pestered, groped, and/or forced to watch college football and *American Pickers*. Life without those knuckleheads just feels weird and wrong—kind of like walking around without a phone.

A loud and often annoying phone. But a phone nonetheless.

In the background, the husband pings with a text, startling me. "I'll be there about 10 tomorrow to pick you up. You finish your book? You ready to come home?"

Yep.

ACKNOWLEDGMENTS

I'd like to thank the talented writers who gave advice and put up with me as I wrote, fussed with, and obsessed over this book: Jerry Zezima, Tracy Beckerman, Kelly Allen, W. Bruce Cameron, Janet Frongillo, Leslie Marinelli, Peggy Zambory, Robin Suttell, Hollis Gillespie, Wade Rouse, Jayne Martin, and many more. I'd also like to thank my wonderful editor and mentor, Jeri Kornegay, who edited *I Love You. Now Go Away* with unparalleled skill, eagle eyes, and gentle direction.

Oceans of gratitude go to writer Wanda Argersinger for asking about the completion of my book so often that I started avoiding her emails. Until I finally didn't. May all of you have a friend who is as big of a pain in the ass as Wanda. You will get shit done.

I'm so grateful to the readers of my blog, column and Huffington Post pieces. Without your encouragement, this book wouldn't exist.

Most of all, I want to thank my amazing, long-suffering husband for his warmth, sense of humor about himself and unwavering belief in me. Thank you too, Laura and Levi, the Princess and the Hobo, for being the lights of my life, and the reluctant subjects of so much of my work. The three of you are very good sports.